THE MEDIEVAL CHURCH

THE
MEDIEVAL CHURCH
Success or Failure?

Edited by **BERNARD S. BACHRACH**
University of Minnesota

HOLT, RINEHART AND WINSTON
New York • Chicago • San Francisco • Atlanta
Dallas • Montreal • Toronto • London • Sydney

Cover illustration: Sculpture from the façade of the Cathedral at Rheims, thirteenth century. A priest is giving Communion to a knight who is preparing to go into battle. A second knight in chain mail and armor stands by. *(Giraudon)*

Copyright © 1972 by Holt, Rinehart and Winston, Inc.
All Rights Reserved
Library of Congress Catalog Card Number: 76-162863
ISBN: 0-03-085185-8
Printed in the United States of America
2 3 4 5   008   9 8 7 6 5 4 3 2 1

CONTENTS

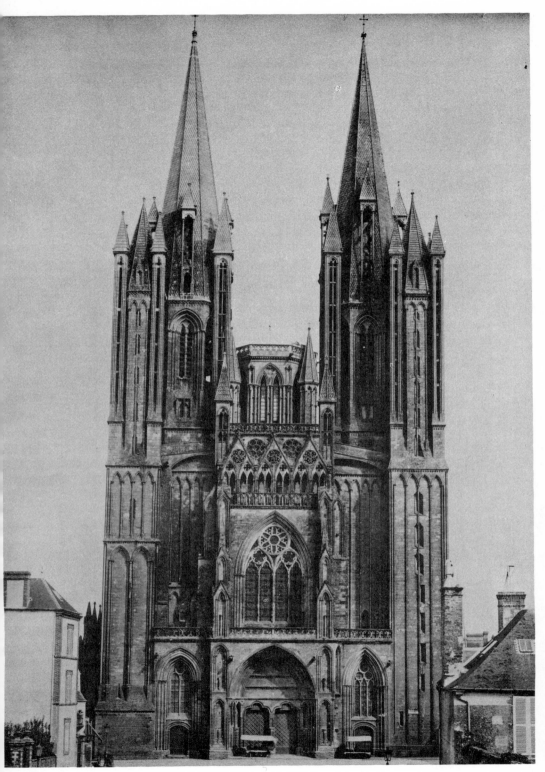

The Cathedral at Coutances, thirteenth century. *(Giraudon)*

INTRODUCTION

During the Middle Ages there was only one Church in Western Europe, the universal Catholic Church of Rome headed by the Pope. Christians who did not adhere to Rome were regarded as heretics and they were persecuted, while outsiders, like the Jews, suffered other severe disadvantages. Since the sixteenth century, however, there have been many Christian churches in Europe and the areas influenced by Western culture. Thus today we rarely speak of the Church.

For a thousand years the Church was the most important institution in Western Europe. All Christians whether emperors or lowly serfs were subject to it throughout their lives. Shortly after birth godparents were chosen for a child and he was baptized. During his early years the child was brought to church and instructed in religion. At about twelve years of age he was confirmed, and throughout his life as a Christian he was expected to confess his sins to a priest. The Christian was also to repent of his sins and do penance imposed upon him by the Church through its clergy. He was expected to take Holy Communion; this, according to theologians, was necessary if he was to be in a state of grace. When a Christian was on his deathbed, he was supposed to receive "last rites" from a priest so that his journey toward salvation would be eased. In order to be married, Christians had to have a priest perform the ceremony, and the "engagement" preceding the marriage had to be announced in church. When a Christian made his will or for that matter participated in any act which required an oath, the Church became involved.

The role played by the Church in religious matters was overshadowed by its role in medieval society in general. In some localities of Western Europe the Church was the largest landholder or landowner, and in other areas it was only one of the more prominent landed elements. Thus the Church not only commanded huge economic resources through its control of land but also controlled the lives of thousands of economic dependents (serfs) who dwelled on its estates. As the lords of huge landed estates Church officials or their representatives administered seigneurial justice. That is, the Church controlled secular courts on the lands it held. It also collected taxes, mustered armed forces, and carried out many other functions usually associated in modern times with secular governments.

On the "international" level the Church, directed by the Pope at Rome, wielded immense power. Popes humbled emperors such as Henry IV, who begged for absolution at Canossa. They initiated and organized major military enterprises such as the Crusades. They deposed kings and tried to establish the Papacy as the feudal overlord of Europe. Through the use of interdicts, excommunications, and the threat of such actions, the Church brought countless numbers of secular magnates to heel. By utilizing its immense economic resources it toppled governments, financed armies, supported banking ventures, and cared for the sick, widows, and orphans.

In every aspect of medieval life the hand of the Church in one form or another can be discerned. Yet the Church had a very inauspicious beginning. For almost three hundred years after Jesus was crucified, Christians living within the Roman Empire were a persecuted minority. They were at times harassed, tortured, and executed for their beliefs and teachings. These beliefs and teachings led them to reject military service and to refuse to worship the deified emperor; these were obligations binding upon every Roman citizen as signs of patriotic loyalty.

By emerging from the status of a persecuted minority to become the dominant religious institution in Western Europe, the Church won a great success. It not only survived against great odds but it overwhelmed its opposition. Yet by the end of the sixteenth century there were many churches in the West. The Church Universal was fragmented by the Reformation; it failed to hold the allegiance of Christians in the West and thus lost much of what it had succeeded in gaining during the Middle Ages.

The great success won by the Church in becoming the official religious institution of Western Europe, a success which for many also signifies the beginning of the Middle Ages, and the failure of the Church which came with the Reformation, a failure which for many marks the end of the Middle Ages, delineate a thousand-year period during which the Church won many successes and suffered many failures. The selections presented in this volume represent the views of eminent scholars who have studied the various activities of the Church in its many fields of endeavor. Yet, the reader must evaluate carefully the remarks of the experts. Each man who writes history, each man who interprets the past, comes to the task with his own preconceived notions, his own biases, and his own limitations. In particular, we must be careful to ascertain whether our experts are judging the success or failure of the Church by the values, aims, and goals espoused by the Church when the events occurred or whether they are making their judgments from the point of view of their own time. And finally, the reader must come to his own evaluation of the medieval Church as a whole as well as of the specific endeavors which it undertook.

The first group of readings deals with the conversion of the barbarians to Christianity. When the Roman Empire in the West was supplanted, the barbarians who succeeded in establishing viable monarchies in its place were for the most part pagans. The great success of the Church in winning them to Christianity is discussed here by Christopher Dawson in a selection from *The Making of Europe*. When the Empire in the West could no longer hold together its erstwhile subjects, who were at that time Christians, and could no longer bring a measure of ancient culture, including religion, to the barbarians, the task was assumed, according to Dawson, by the Pope at Rome. The outstanding figure in the drive to convert the barbarians was Pope Gregory I, called the Great. With the help of missionaries like Augustine of Canterbury, but especially through the assistance of wandering Celtic monks from the British Isles, much of Germany was brought into the Christian world. Monasteries were established throughout the West, and these institutions played an essential role in making Europe Christian by providing centers of religion and culture.

Dawson notes that the religion practiced by the newly converted barbarians was a syncretism of paganism and Christianity in which the old spirits of the woods and rocks fused with the Trinity and the saints. The primitive nature of Christianity as practiced by the masses is the subject of the selection from *The Legends of the Saints* by Hippolyte Delehaye. Father Delehaye shows that Christians in the Middle Ages were hardly unique in concocting puerile religious stories or in confusing and confounding reality by creating legends. It is Father Delehaye's contention that the ignorant masses have always and will continue to create legends because their standards of truth and comprehension of reality are severely limited and do not even approach the level demanded by the serious historian. We must ask, however, whether the Church failed because it did not provide the means by which Christians could shed the ignorance and superstition which marked pagan practices and came to permeate the teachings of elements within the Church itself.

The quality of Christianity and of the Church is of primary importance in the selection from Heinrich Fichtenau's *Carolingian Empire*. Fichtenau argues that a Christian ideal and an esteemed church to which all levels of society could dedicate themselves were essential to the preservation and the success of the Carolingian Empire. In the Carolingian Empire, however, and especially in its eastern, Germanic half, the Church was in lay hands. Petty magnates owned the churches located on their lands and often installed illiterate serfs as local priests. At the higher levels of society bishops and abbots were chosen by emperors, kings, and other less important rulers whose political and family interests dominated at the expense of the Church. According to Fichtenau the upper classes regarded the Church and its servants with contempt. Many clerics were serfs who had been forced into the priesthood, and no cleric was permitted to bear arms, the only means by which true honor in Germanic terms could be obtained. Religion was neglected by illiterate, servile, ignorant, drunken, and disinterested clerics. Paganism flourished among clergy and populace alike. This degraded state of the Carolingian church, according to Fichtenau, was due in part at least to the failure of those who exercised power to try to eradicate ancient Germanic practices which impinged upon the Church.

The second group of readings deals with the growing power and prestige of the Church in Western Europe. Reform of the Church was the goal of a small but effective minority of dedicated clerics who sought to free ecclesiastical institutions from lay control after the fall of the Carolingian Empire. By the mid-eleventh century Church reformers had gained considerable strength and power in their "struggle for right order in the world." In the selection from *Church, State, and Christian Society at the Time of the Investiture Contest* Gerd Tellenbach discusses the program worked out by the reformers in their attempt to establish the "right order." (The wrong order as perceived by the reformers is described in the previous selection.) The reformers attempted to deprive the laity of spiritual functions and strove to ensure that each church had sufficient income to meet its needs. This program led to an attack on fundamental and time-honored institutions such as lay investiture, proprietary churches, and non-canonical election of bishops and abbots. Lay control of clerical appointments meant that ecclesiastical wealth was to a great extent under secular control. By striking at lay control of ecclesiastical wealth the reformers precipitated a conflict that led to the deposition of emperors and the excommunication of influential but traditionally minded clerics.

The reformers' battle to be masters in their own house enhanced the prestige of the Church throughout the West. As a partial result of this increased prestige, Pope Urban II was able to preach and launch a holy war against the Muslims for the purpose of regaining the holy places of the East, especially Jerusalem. Thousands of Christians, rich and poor alike, joined the First Crusade against the infidel. During the next three centuries or so many more crusades were preached by the Church, organized by the papacy, and led by papal legates. Some of them were directed against Muslims, but others were aimed at destroying Christians like the Emperor Frederick II. In the selection from *A History of the Crusades,* Steven Runciman concentrates on the first two centuries of crusading. In his judgment the Crusades accomplished little of what they set out to do and probably caused more harm than good.

Among the many Christians who went on the Crusades were thousands of noble fighting men, knights. These warriors, who played an important role in the warfare of feudal Europe, are said by some scholars to have lived acording to a chivalric code. In *French Chivalry,* Sidney Painter examines the relation between the chivalric ideal and everyday reality. The selection from it presented here deals with religious chivalry and the attempt by the Church to impose Christian restraint on the lusty brawlers who were the knights of feudal Europe. Crusading orders like the Templars were supposed to draw knights who lived like monks; the Truce and Peace of God made it legal to fight only on certain days of the week while forbidding combat on other days, and attempted to exclude certain classes of society from the perils of warfare. Important clerics like John of Salisbury and Ramón Lull wrote learned tracts pointing out the religious elements and obligations of knighthood. It is doubtful, however, that a religio-ethical code of behavior ever came to dominate the everyday life of the average European knight.

Unlike the Crusades, which came to an unheroic end after some three centuries of futility, the universities, which were also a child of the medieval Church, have had general success for some seven centuries. From the fall of the Roman Empire until the emergence of the modern world, education at all levels was carried on for the most part by clerics. The monastic schools, which bore the burden of preserving classical manuscripts and educating the relatively few literate souls of the early Middle Ages, were superseded by the cathedral schools during the early years of medieval Europe's revival. In the twelfth century the focus of higher education began to turn from the cathedral schools, which were dominated by bishops, to universities, which were controlled at least in part by the papacy. In the selection from *The Rise of Universities*, Charles Homer Haskins discusses university development in northern Europe. Paris, according to Haskins, was the model university, and it held the premier place throughout Europe in the study and teaching of theology, the queen of the sciences.

The third group of readings deals with the later Middle Ages, during which the efforts of the previous periods bore their fruit. All the great enterprises supported by the medieval Church, such as the reform movement, crusading, and education, cost great sums of money. Also in its day-to-day activities, such as caring for the poor and running hospitals, the Church incurred large expenses. Although it was one of the richest institutions in medieval Europe, the Church needed credit financing from the twelfth through the sixteenth century. It could hardly function solely as an economic institution, however, for it was also the repository of moral teaching on all aspects of human endeavor. In the selection from *The Church and Economic Activity in the Middle Ages*, John Gilchrist examines the relation between the Church's teachings on economic matters and its own economic behavior. He shows how it was not possible for the Church as an economic institution to live up to the moral standards it established as a religious institution. He exposes the institutional contradictions which forced it to go against its own teachings, and the human failings of the men who were allotted the task of doing God's work on earth.

The contradictions between the Church's teachings and its activities brought about considerable disillusionment at all levels of medieval society, but especially among the lower classes. In the selection from *The Medieval Scene*, George Gordon Coulton describes popular religious feelings in the later Middle Ages and contrasts them with the activities of the Church. He argues that many of the Church's institutions incurred the hostility of the common man. The Inquisition, for example, with its strict judicial procedures and scholastic arguments, is pointed to as the very antithesis of popular religious feeling with its mysticism and superstition.

Despite their growing disillusionment with Church institutions, the people of medieval Europe were profoundly influenced by religion. In *The Waning of the Middle Ages,* Johan Huizinga describes how popular religiosity distorted and cheapened religion. According to him religion was of great importance, but its mysteries and complexities could not be assimilated by the great mass of medieval people; they found it necessary to portray the intangibles of religion with images, and for them the image became the reality. The permeation of society by religiosity led also to the seeing of religious symbols in mundane matters; thus even the meanest human activities were often seen to have a religious meaning. Religion was in this way cheapened and made to be far less than the Church taught it to be.

The question of the success or failure of the medieval Church can be approached in many ways. We may evaluate movements like the Crusades or institutions like the universities and then draw up a balance sheet, always being careful to indicate whether we are employing medieval or modern criteria in our judgment. We may, however, delve more deeply into the problem of success or failure in the hope of gaining a more fundamental understanding. For example, questions were raised in several of the selections concerning the meaning of religion to the great mass of Christians. From this point of inquiry it seems that the Church may have succeeded all too well in making Europe Christian. For in doing this a milieu was created in which the vast majority of people, because of lack of education and natural limitations, simply could not measure up. In short, by making all Europe Christian and asking more of people than they could comprehend or give, did the Church succeed in ensuring its own failure?

In the reprinted selections footnotes appearing in the original sources have in general been omitted unless they contribute to the argument or better understanding of the selection.

Among the many attempts to characterize the essence of European civilization in the Early Middle Ages, *The Making of Europe* by CHRISTOPHER DAWSON (b. 1889) merits an important place. The efforts of Gibbon and others who followed him to show that Christianity and barbarism brought an end to the glories of the ancient world are opposed by Dawson, who attempts to demonstrate that the Church and the barbarians forged a new and very worthwhile culture, our own.*

Christopher Dawson

Europe Becomes Christian

The fall of the Western Empire in the fifth century did not result in the immediate formation of an independent cultural unity in Western Europe. In the sixth century Western Christendom was still dependent on the Eastern Empire, and Western culture was a chaotic mixture of barbarian and Roman elements which as yet possessed no spiritual unity and no internal principle of social order. The temporary revival of civilisation in the sixth century was followed by a second period of decline and barbarian invasion which reduced European culture to a far lower level than it had reached in the fifth century. Once again it was on the Danube that the crisis developed. The second half of the reign of Justinian had seen a progressive weakening of the frontier defences and the Balkan provinces were exposed to a series of destructive invasions. The Gepids, an East German people allied to the Goths, had taken the place of the Ostrogoths in Pannonia, while the Kotrigur Huns held the lower Danube and carried their raids to the very gates of Constantinople. In their wake came the Slavs, who now for the first time emerge from the prehistoric obscurity that envelops their origins. Faced by so many dangers, the imperial government found itself unable to defend its frontiers by military means and fell back upon diplomacy. It egged on the Utigurs

*From Christopher Dawson, *The Making of Europe* (New York: Meridian Books, 1956), pp. 169–186. Reprinted by permission of The Society of Authors as the literary representative of the estate of Christopher Dawson. Footnotes omitted.

of the Kuban steppe to attack the Kotri-
gurs, the Herules and the Lombards
against the Gepids, and the Avars against
the Gepids and the Slavs. Thus in 567,
after the death of Justinian, the Avars
united with the Lombards to destroy the
Gepid kingdom, and the government of
Justin II, hoping to recover Sirmium for
the Empire, left the Gepids to their fate.
But here the Byzantines overreached
themselves, for Bayan, the great Khan of
the Avars, was no petty chieftain to be
made the catspaw of imperial diplomacy,
but a ruthless Asiatic conqueror of the
type of Attila and Genghis Khan. In place
of a relatively stable Germanic state, the
Empire now had to deal with a people of
warlike nomads whose empire extended
from the Adriatic to the Baltic. Under
its pressure the Danube frontier finally
gave way, and the Illyrian provinces,
which had been for nearly four hundred
years the foundation of the military
strength of the Empire and the cradle of
its soldiers and rulers, were occupied by
Slavonic peoples who were dependent on
the Avars.

But the Empire was not the only power
to suffer. All Central Europe fell a prey
to the Asiatic conquerors. Their raids
extended as far as the frontiers of the
Frankish kingdom. The Northern Sueves
were forced to evacuate the lands between
the Elbe and the Oder, and Eastern Germany was colonised by the Slavonic
subjects of the Avars. Thus of the East
German peoples who had formerly ruled
Eastern Europe from the Baltic to the
Black Sea, there remained only the Lombards, and they were too wise to try
conclusions with their Asiatic allies.
Immediately after the fall of the Gepid
Kingdom they evacuated their lands on
the Danube and marched on Italy. Here
again the Empire was powerless to protect
its subjects. Lombardy and the whole of

the interior of the peninsula was occupied
by the invaders, and the Byzantines only
preserved their hold upon the coastal
districts—the Venetian Islands, Ravenna
and the Pentapolis, the Duchy of Rome,
and Genoa, Amalfi and Naples.

This was the last blow to the declining
civilisation of Italy, and we cannot wonder that to the men of that age the end of
all things seemed at hand. The writings of
St. Gregory the Great reflect the appalling sufferings and the profound pessi-
mism of the age. He even welcomes the
pestilence that was devastating the West
as a refuge from the horrors that surrounded him. "When we consider the way
in which other men have died we find a
solace in reflecting on the form of death
that threatens us. What mutilations, what
cruelties have we seen inflicted upon men,
for which death is the only cure and in
the midst of which life was a torture!"
He sees Ezekiel's prophecy of the seething
pot fulfilled in the fate of Rome: "Of this
city it is well said 'The meat is boiled
away and the bones in the midst thereof.' . . . For where is the Senate? Where
is the People? The bones are all dissolved,
the flesh is consumed, all the pomp of
the dignities of this world is gone. The
whole mass is boiled away."

"Yet even we who remain, few as we
are, still are daily smitten with the sword,
still are daily crushed by innumerable
afflictions. Therefore let it be said, 'Set
the pot also empty upon the coals.' For
the Senate is no more, and the People
has perished, yet sorrow and sighing
are multiplied daily among the few that
are left. Rome is, as it were, already empty
and burning. But what need is there to
speak of men when, as the work of ruin
spreads, we see the very buildings perish-
ing. Wherefore it is fitly added concerning the city already empty, 'Let the brass
thereof be hot and melt.' Already the pot

itself is being consumed in which were first consumed the flesh and the bones. . . ."

But the worst had not yet come. In the seventh century the Arabs conquered Byzantine Africa, the most civilised province of the West, and the great African Church, the glory of Latin Christianity, disappears from history. Early in the eighth century the tide of Moslem invasion swept over Christian Spain and threatened Gaul itself. Christendom had become an island isolated between the Moslem south and the Barbarian north.

Yet it was in this age of universal ruin and destruction that the foundations of the new Europe were being laid by men like St. Gregory, who had no idea of building up a new social order but who laboured for the salvation of men in a dying world because the time was short. And it was just this indifference to temporal results which gave the Papacy the power to become a rallying-point for the forces of life in the general decadence of European civilisation. In the words of the inscription which Pope John III set up in the Church of the Most Holy Apostles: "In a straitened age, the Pope showed himself more generous and disdained to be cast down though the world failed."

At the very moment of the fall of the Empire in the West, St. Augustine, in his great book *Of the City of God,* had set forth the programme which was to inspire the ideals of the new age. He viewed all history as the evolution of two opposite principles embodied in two hostile societies, the heavenly and the earthly cities, Sion and Babylon, the Church and the World. The one had no final realisation on earth, it was *"in via,"* its *patria* was heavenly and eternal; the other found its realisation in earthly prosperity, in the wisdom and glory of man; it was its own end and its own justification. The State, it is true, was not condemned as such. In

so far as it was Christian, it subserved the ends of the heavenly city. But it was a subordinate society, the servant and not the master: it was the spiritual society that was supreme. The moment that the state came into conflict with the higher power, the moment that it set itself up as an end in itself, it became identified with the earthly city and lost all claims to a higher sanction than the law of force and self-interest. Without justice, what is a great kingdom but a great robbery — *magnum latrocinium?* Conquering or being conquered does no one either good or harm. It is pure waste of energy, the game of fools for an empty prize. The terrestrial world is unsubstantial and transitory, the only reality worth striving for is that which is eternal — the heavenly Jerusalem — "the vision of peace."

This ideal of the supremacy and independence of the spiritual power found its organ of expression above all in the Papacy. Already before the fall of the Empire the Roman bishop possessed a unique position as the successor and representative of St. Peter. Rome was the "Apostolic See" *par excellence,* and in virtue of this authority it had intervened decisively against both Constantinople and Alexandria in the doctrinal struggles of the fourth and fifth centuries. The decline of the Empire in the West naturally enhanced its prestige, for the process by which the bishop became the representative of the Roman tradition in the conquered provinces was far more accentuated in the case of the ancient capital. The old imperial tradition was carried over into the sphere of religion. In the fifth century St. Leo the Great, addressing his people on the Feast of SS. Peter and Paul, could say, "These are they, who have brought thee to such glory as a holy nation, a chosen people, a royal and priestly city that thou mightest be made the head of the world by the Holy See of St. Peter, and mightest bear rule more widely by divine religion than by earthly dominion."

The Pope was still a loyal subject of the Emperor and regarded the cause of the Empire as inseparable from that of the Christian religion. The Liturgy couples together "the foes of the Roman name and the enemies of the Catholic Faith," and the Roman Missal still contains a prayer for the Roman Empire "that God may subdue to the Emperor all the barbarous nations, to our perpetual peace." But after the Lombard invasion and the age of St. Gregory, the actual authority of the imperial government in Italy was reduced to a shadow, and it was on the Pope that the responsibility fell for the safety of Rome and the feeding of its inhabitants. Rome became, like Venice or Cherson, a kind of semi-independent member of the Byzantine state. It remained an open door between the civilised East and the barbarised West; it was a common meeting-ground to both, without exactly belonging to either.

This anomalous position was very favourable to the exercise of papal influence in the barbaric kingdoms of the West, since the Papacy enjoyed the prestige of its connection with the Eastern Empire without any danger of being considered an instrument of imperial policy, and thus the Frankish kings raised no objection to the Bishop of Arles receiving the office of Apostolic Vicar for the Church in Gaul. Nevertheless, the power of the Papacy, and with it that of the Universal Church, was greatly limited by the inherent weakness of the local churches. The Church of the Frankish kingdom, especially, suffered from the same process of barbarisation and cultural decadence that affected the whole society.

The bishop became a territorial magnate, like the count, and the greater was his wealth and power, the greater was the danger of the secularisation of the office. The monarchy had no direct intention of interfering with the prerogatives of the Church, but it naturally claimed the right of appointing to an office which took such an important share in the administration of the kingdom, and its candidates were often of very dubious character, like the "robber bishops," Salonius and Sagittarius, whose exploits are described by Gregory of Tours. . . . Moreover, the transformation of the state into an agrarian society and the progressive decline of the city had a most deleterious effect on the Church, since the influence of the barbarous and half pagan countryside came to predominate over that of the cities. For while in the East Christianity had penetrated the countryside from the first, and the peasantry was, if anything, more Christian than the townspeople, in Western Europe the Church had grown up in the towns and so had failed to make a deep impression on the peasants and countryfolk. They were *pagani*, the "pagans," who clung after the manner of peasants to their immemorial customs and beliefs, to the rites of seedtime and harvest, and to the venerations of their sacred trees and springs.

Yet the fundamental ethos of the new religion was in no way alien to the peasant life. Its first beginning had been amongst the fishermen and peasants of Galilee, and the Gospel teaching is full of the imagery of the field and the fold and the vineyard. Christianity only needed a new organ besides the city episcopate in order to permeate the countryside. Now at the very moment when the conversion of the Empire was binding the Church closer to the urban polity, a new movement was drawing men away from the city. The heroes of the second age of Christianity, the successors of the martyrs, were the ascetics—the men who deliberately cut themselves off from the whole inheritance of city culture in order to live a life of labour and prayer under the simplest possible conditions.

In the fourth century the deserts of Egypt and Syria were peopled with colonies of monks and hermits which became schools of the religious life for all the provinces of the Empire, and the neighbouring peoples of the East. But in the West, though its fundamental ideals were the same, the difference of social conditions forced the monasteries to take up a different attitude towards the society that surrounded them.

In the rural districts of the West the monastery was the only centre of Christian life and teaching, and it was upon the monks rather than upon the bishops and their clergy that the task of converting the heathen or semi-heathen peasant population ultimately fell. This is evident even as early as the fourth century in the life of the founder of Gallic monasticism, the great Martin of Tours, but its great development was due to the work of John Cassian, who brought Gaul into direct contact with the tradition of the monks of the Egyptain desert, and to St. Honoratus, the founder of Lerins, which became the greatest monastic centre of Western Europe in the fifth century and the source of a far-reaching influence.

But it was in the newly-converted Celtic lands of the far West that the influence of monasticism became all-important. The beginnings of the monastic movement in this region dates from the fifth century, and probably owes its origins to the influence of Lerins, where St. Patrick had studied in the years before his apostolate and where in 433 a British monk, Faustus, had held the position of abbot. But though St. Patrick had introduced the monastic life into Ireland, his

organisation of the Church followed the traditional lines of episcopal organisation, as did that of the British Church in Wales. Since, however, the Roman bishop was always the bishop of a city, the normal system of ecclesiastical organisation possessed no natural social basis in the Celtic lands, where the social unit was not the city but the tribe. Consequently, the great extension of monastic influence and culture in the sixth century led to the monastery's taking the place of the bishopric as the centre of ecclesiastical life and organisation. The movement started in South Wales, where the monastery of St. Illtyd on Caldey Island became a great school of the monastic life after the model of Lerins early in the sixth century. From this centre the monastic revival was diffused throughout western Britain and Brittany by the work of St. Samson, St. Cadoc of Llancarvan, St. Gildas and St. David. Moreover, the great development of Irish monasticism that took place in the sixth century under the "Saints of the Second Order" was closely related to this movement. St. Finnian of Clonard (d. 549), the chief inaugurator of the new type of monasticism, was in close relations with St. Cadoc of Llancarvan and with St. Gildas, and it was through him and his disciples, above all St. Ciaran of Clonmacnoise (d. 549), St. Brendan of Clonfert, and St. Columba of Derry and Iona, that the monastic tradition of St. Illtyd and his school was diffused in Ireland. The importance of this movement was literary as well as ascetic, for the school of St. Illtyd and St. Cadoc cultivated the traditions of the old schools of rhetoric, as well as those of purely ecclesiastical learning, and encouraged the study of classical literature.

This is the origin of the movement of culture which produced the great monastic schools of Clonard and Clonmacnoise and Bangor, and made Ireland the leader of Western culture from the close of the sixth century. It is, however, probable that its development also owes something to native traditions, for the Irish, unlike the other barbaric peoples, possessed a native tradition of learning, represented by the schools of the poets or *Filid,* which enjoyed considerable wealth and social prestige. The new monastic schools entered in a sense into the inheritance of this native tradition, and were able to replace the old druidic and bardic schools as the intellectual organs of Irish society. By degrees the imported classical culture of the Christian monasteries was blended with the native literary tradition, and there arose a new vernacular literature inspired in part by Christian influence but founded in part on native pagan traditions. Although this literature has come down to us mainly through Middle Irish versions of mediaeval date, there can be no doubt that its original creation goes back to the seventh and eighth centuries—the Golden Age of Irish Christian culture—and that the literary tradition of mediaeval Ireland has its roots deep in the prehistoric past. The most striking example of this is the great prose epic or saga—the *Tain Bo Cualgne*—which takes us back behind the Middle Age and behind the classical tradition to the heroic age of Celtic culture, and preserves the memory of a stage of society resembling that of the Homeric world. Thus there was no sudden break between the old barbaric tradition and that of the Church, such as occurred elsewhere, and a unique fusion took place between the Church and the Celtic tribal society entirely unlike anything else in Western Europe. The hierarchic episcopal organisation of the Church, which was common to the rest of Christendom, was here completely subordinated to the monastic system. Bishops of course continued to exist and to confer orders, but they were no longer the rulers of the Church. The monasteries were not only the great centres of religious and intellectual life; they were also centres of ecclesiastical jurisdiction. The abbot was the ruler of a diocese or *paroechia,* and usually kept one or more bishops in his community to perform the necessary episcopal functions, except in those cases in which he was a bishop himself. Still more extraordinary is the fact that this kind of quasi-episcopal jurisdiction was sometimes exercised by women, for the see of Kildare was a dependency of St. Bridget's great monastery and was ruled jointly by bishop and abbess, so that it was in the phrase of her biographer "a see at once episcopal and virginal."

The monasteries were closely connected with the tribal society, for it was the prevailing if not the universal custom for the abbot to be chosen from the clan to which the founder belonged. Thus the *Book of Armagh* records in the ninth century that the Church of Trim had been ruled for nine generations by the descendants of the chieftain who endowed the see in the days of St. Patrick. In the same way the early abbots of Iona belonged to the family of St. Columba, the royal race of the northern Ui Niall.

In organisation and way of life the Irish monks closely resembled their Egyptian prototypes. They rivalled the monks of the desert in the rigour of their discipline and the asceticism of their life. Their monasteries were not great buildings like the later Benedictine abbeys, but consisted of groups of huts and small oratories, like the Egyptian laura, and were surrounded by a *rath* or earthwork. Moreover, they preserved the oriental idea of the eremitical life as the culmination and goal of the monastic state. In Ireland, however, this ideal assumed a peculiar form that is not found elsewhere. It was common for monks to devote themselves to a life of voluntary exile and pilgrimage. The case recorded in the Anglo-Saxon Chronicle (*s.a.* 891) of the three monks "who stole away from Ireland in a boat without any oars because they would live in a state of pilgrimage for the love of God, they recked not where," is typical of this development. It led to a movement of travel and exploration which is reflected in a legendary form in the adventures of St. Brendan the Navigator. When the Vikings first discovered Iceland they found that the Irish "papas" had been there before them, and every island of the northern seas had its colony of ascetics. The informants of Dicuil, the Carolingian geographer, had even sailed beyond Iceland and reached the frozen Arctic seas.

But the real importance of this movement lies in the impulse that it gave to missionary activity, and it was as missionaries that the Celtic monks made their most important contribution to European culture. The monastic colonies of St. Columba at Iona, and of his namesake Columbanus at Luxeuil, were the starting points of a great expansion of Christianity. To the one was due the conversion of Scotland and of the Northumbrian kingdom, to the other the revival of monasticism and the conversion of the remaining pagan elements in the Frankish kingdom. Luxeuil, with its six hundred monks, became the monastic metropolis of Western Europe, and the centre of a great colonising and missionary activity. Very many of the great mediaeval monasteries not only of France, but of Flanders and Germany, owe their foundation to its work—for example, Jumièges, St. Vandrille, Solignac and Corbie in France, Stavelot and Malmedy in Belgium, St.

Gall and Dissentis in Switzerland, and Bobbio, the last foundation of Columbanus himself, in Italy. All through Central Europe the wandering Irish monks have left their traces, and the German Church still honours the names of St. Kilian, St. Gall, St. Fridolin and St. Corbinian among its founders.

It is easy to understand what an influence this movement must have exercised on the peasants. It was essentially rural, avoiding the towns, and seeking the wildest regions of forest and mountain. Far more than the preaching of bishop and priest from the distant city, the presence of these colonies of black-robed ascetics must have impressed the peasant mind with the sense of a new power that was stronger than the nature spirits of the old peasant religion. Moreover, the Irish monks were themselves countrymen with a deep feeling for nature and for the wild things. The biographer of Columban relates how, as he went through the forest, the squirrels and the birds would come to be caressed by him, and "would frisk about and gambol in great delight, like puppies fawning on their master." Indeed, the legends of the monastic saints are full of an almost Franciscan feeling for nature. It is true that the Celtic monastic ideal was that of the desert; they loved the forest or, better still, uninhabited and inaccessible islands, like Skellig Michael, one of the most impressive of monastic sites, just as the Eastern monks to-day still choose Mount Athos or the Meteora. Nevertheless, the monastic settlements were forced by necessity to take up the peasants' task, to clear the forest and to till the ground. The lives of the monastic saints of the Merovingian period, whether Gallic or Celtic, are full of references to their agricultural labours— their work of clearing the forest and of bringing back to cultivation the lands that had been abandoned during the period of the invasions. Many of them, like St. Walaric, the founder of St. Valery-sur-Somme, were themselves of peasant origin. Others, though noble by birth, spent their whole lives working as peasants, like St. Theodulph, the abbot of St. Thierry near Rheims, who would never cease from labour and whose plough was hung up in the church as a relic by the peasants.

These were the men to whom the conversion of the peasants was really due, for they stood so near to the peasant culture that they were able to infuse it with the spirit of the new religion. It was through them that the cultus that had been paid to the spirits of nature was transferred to the Saints. The sacred wells, the sacred trees and the sacred stones retained the devotion of the people, but they were consecrated to new powers, and acquired new associations. The peasants near Rheims paid honour to a holy tree, which was said to have sprung miraculously from the ox-goad which the same St. Theodulph thrust into the earth. In the West the stone crosses of the saints replaced the menhirs of the heathen cult, just as the great tumulus of Carnac has been crowned by a chapel of St. Michael, and a dolmen at Ploucret has been turned into a chapel of the Seven Saints. It was only with difficulty that the Church succeeded in putting down the old pagan customs, and it was usually done by providing a Christian ceremony to take the place of the heathen one. The statement in the *Liber Pontificalis* that St. Leo instituted the ceremonies of Candlemas in order to put an end to the Lupercalia is perhaps erroneous, but the Great Litanies and processions of April 25th seem to have taken the place of the Robigalia, and the feast of the Collection or *Oblatio* that of the opening of the Ludi Apollinares.

Still more remarkable is the correspondence between the Ember Days and the seasonal pagan Feriae of the harvest, the vintage and the seedtime. The liturgy for the Advent Ember Days, especially, is full of references to the seedtime, which it associates with the mystery of the Divine Birth. "The Divine seed descends, and whereas the fruits of the field support our earthly life, this seed from on high gives our soul the Food of Immortality. The earth has yielded its corn, wine and oil, and now the ineffable Birth approaches of Him who through His mercy bestows the Bread of Life upon the Sons of God."

But this liturgical transfiguration of the spirit of the Vegetation Religion was too spiritual to reach the mind of the peasant. In spite of all the efforts of the Church the old pagan rites still survived and all through Europe the peasants continued to light the midsummer fires on St. John's Eve and to practise the magic ritual of fertility in spring. Even to-day, as Maurice Barrès has shown in *La Colline Inspirée*, the sinister powers of the old nature religion are still latent in the European countryside and are apt to reassert themselves whenever the control of the new order is relaxed. Nevertheless it is remarkable that it is just in those regions where the external survivals of pagan customs are most noticeable, as in Brittany and the Tirol, that the Christian ethos has affected the life of the peasant most deeply. For Christianity did succeed in remoulding the peasant culture. The old gods disappeared and their holy places were reconsecrated to the saints of the new religion. It is true that the cult of the local sanctuaries and their pilgrimages gave occasion to all kinds of strange survivals, as we see in the Breton Pardons to this day. But it was this very continuity of culture—this association of the old with the new—which opened the peasant mind to Christian influences that it could not receive in any other way. And the disappearance of the old peasant customs in later times has often been accompanied by a relapse into paganism of a far deeper kind than the paganism of archaeological survivals.

But the evangelisation of rural Europe during the Merovingian period is only one among the services which monasticism rendered to European civilisation. It was also destined to be the chief agent of the Papacy in its task of ecclesiastical reform and to exert a vital influence on the political and cultural restoration of European society. The same period that saw the rise of Celtic monasticism in Ireland was also marked by a new development of monasticism in Italy which was to have an even greater historical importance. This was due to the work of St. Benedict "the Patriarch of the Monks of the West," who founded the monastery of Monte Cassino about the year 520. It was he who first applied the Latin genius for order and law to the monastic institution and who completed that socialisation of the monastic life which had been begun by St. Pachomius and St. Basil. The ideal of the monks of the desert was that of individual asceticism and their monasteries were communities of hermits. That of the Benedictine was essentially co-operative and social: its aim was not to produce heroic feats of asceticism, but the cultivation of the common life, "the school of the service of the Lord." In comparison with the rules of Pachomius and St. Columban, that of St. Benedict appears moderate and easy, but it involved a much higher degree of organisation and stability. The Benedictine monastery was a state in miniature with a settled hierarchy and constitution and an organised economic life. From the first it was a land-owning corporation which possessed villas and serfs and vineyards, and the monastic economy occupies a larger place in the rule of St. Benedict than in any of the earlier rules. Hence the importance of co-operative labour which filled so large a part of the life of the Benedictine monk, for St. Benedict was inspired by the ideals which St. Augustine had set forth in his treatise *De opere monachorum* and had an equal detestation of the idle and "gyrovagous" monks who had done so much to bring monasticism into disrepute in the West.

But the primary duty of the monk was not manual labour, but prayer, above all the common recitation of the Divine Office, which St. Benedict terms "the work of God." Nor was study neglected. It was the monasteries which kept alive the classical tradition after the fall of the Empire. In fact the last representative in the West of the learned tradition of the Roman civil service—Cassiodorus—was also a founder of monasteries and the author of the first programme of monastic studies. It is true that the ostentatious literary culture of the old rhetorician at Vivarium was alien from the stern simplicity and spirituality which inspired the Benedictine rule, but Western monasticism was to inherit both traditions. Under the influence of the Papacy the rule of St. Benedict became the Roman standard of the monastic life and finally the universal type of Western monasticism. After the Celtic expansion came the Latin organisation.

The beginning of this Benedictine world mission was due to the action of St. Gregory, himself a Benedictine monk. It was from the Benedictine monastery on the Caelian that St. Augustine and his monks set out on their mission for the conversion of England, and the Benedictine monastery at Canterbury, probably the earliest Benedictine foundation outside Italy, became the starting point of a movement of religious organisation and unification which created a new centre of Christian civilisation in the West.

The appearance of the new Anglo-Saxon culture of the seventh century is perhaps the most important event between the age of Justinian and that of Charlemagne, for it reacted with profound effect on the whole continental development. In its origins it was equally indebted to the two forces that we have described — the Celtic monastic movement and the Roman Benedictine mission. Northern England was common ground to them both, and it was here that the new Christian culture arose in the years between 650 and 680 owing to the interaction and fusion of the two different elements. Christianity had been introduced into Northumbria by the Roman Paulinus who baptised King Edwin in 627 and established the metropolitan see at the old Roman city of York, but the defeat of Edwin by the heathen Penda and the Welsh Cadwallon led to the temporary ruin of the Anglian Church. It was re-established by King Oswald in 634 with the help of St. Aidan and the Celtic missionaries whom he brought from Iona to Lindisfarne, and throughout his reign Celtic influence reigned supreme. It was not until the synod of Whitby in 664 that the Roman party finally triumphed, owing to the intervention of St. Wilfrid, who dedicated his long and stormy life to the service of the Roman unity. It is to him and to his friend and fellow-worker, St. Benedict Biscop, that the establishment of Benedictine monasticism in Northern England is due. Nor was their activity solely of ecclesiastical importance; for they were the missionaries of culture as well as of religion, and they were responsible for the rise of the new Anglian art.

They brought back from their many journeys to Rome and Gaul skilled craftsmen and architects, as well as books, pictures, vestments and musicians, and their abbeys of Ripon and Hexham, Wearmouth and Jarrow, were the great centres of the new culture. At the same time in the South, a similar work was being carried out by the Greek-Syrian archbishop, Theodore, and the African abbot, Hadrian, who were sent from Rome in 668. In them we can trace the appearance of a new wave of higher culture from the East, which does much to explain the rise of Anglo-Saxon scholarship and the superiority of the Latin of Bede and Alcuin to the barbarous style of Gregory of Tours or the Celtic author of the *Hisperica Famina*. The higher culture had survived far more in the Byzantine provinces of Africa and the East, and the storm of Arab invasion had brought an influx of refugees to the West, who played somewhat the same part in the seventh century as the Greek refugees from Constantinople in the fifteenth. From 685 to 752 the Roman see was occupied by a succession of Greeks and Syrians, many of them men of considerable character, and the oriental influence was at its height, not only at Rome but throughout the West. In the Anglian art of this period, the oriental influence is especially well marked. From about the year 670 — probably as a result of the activity of Benedict Biscop — we find in place of the old Germanic art, a new school of sculpture and decoration, purely oriental in inspiration, and based on the Syrian motive of a vinescroll interwoven with the figures of birds or beasts, as we see it in the great series of Anglian crosses, especially the famous ones at Ruthwell and Bewcastle, which probably date from the beginning of the eighth century. That an Irish school of art also existed in Northumbria is proved by the magnificent

Lindisfarne Book of Gospels, but there is no trace of its influence on architecture or sculpture. On the other hand the art of Saxon England is much more composite and shows the influence not only of the oriental style both in its Northumbrian and its Frankish Merovingian forms, but also that of Irish art.

Nevertheless, behind all these foreign influences there lies a foundation of native culture. The same age and district that produced the Anglian crosses also saw the rise of Anglo-Saxon literature. It was the age in which the old pagan story of Beowulf received its literary form, and even more characteristic of the time were the Christian poets, Caedmon, the shepherd of Whitby Abbey, whose romantic story is preserved by Bede, and Cynewulf, the author of several surviving poems, including *Andreas, Elene, Juliana* and, perhaps, also of the noble *Dream of the Rood,* a quotation from which is sculptured on the Ruthwell cross.

The rise of this vernacular literature no doubt owes something to the influence of Ireland where, as we have seen, a remarkable development of vernacular Christian culture was taking place at this time. But Anglo-Saxon literature has a very distinctive character which is neither Celtic nor Teutonic but all its own. It is marked by a characteristic melancholy which has nothing in common with the "Celtic melancholy" of literary tradition. It is the melancholy of a people living among the ruins of a dead civilisation whose thoughts dwell on the glories of the past and the vanity of human achievement.

But this native tradition is not necessarily Anglo-Saxon: it may go back further than that. Mr. Collingwood has explained the sudden flowering of Anglian art as due to a renaissance of the genius of the conquered people, and this seems even more probable in the case of the leaders

of religion and culture. The almost entire absence of any remains of heathen Anglian settlements north of the Tees in Bernicia, the centre of Northumbrian power in the days of St. Oswald, is specially noteworthy. It suggests the probability of the survival of native elements in the very region that played so large a part in the history of the Anglian culture, *i.e.,* Tyneside and the east end of the Roman wall.

And the same holds good to a lesser degree of Wessex, both Aldhelm and Boniface being natives of regions not occupied by the Saxons in early times. The enthusiasm of the newly converted Anglo-Saxons for the Latin culture and the Roman order cannot have been merely fortuitous. A man like Bede, who represents the highest level of culture in the West between the fall of the Empire and the ninth century, cannot have been an artificial product of an Italian mission to Germanic barbarians; the appearance of such a type in Denmark, for example, even after its conversion, is inconceivable. The conversion of the Anglo-Saxons produced such a vital change in England because it meant the reassertion of the old cultural tradition after the temporary victory of barbarism. It was the return of Britain to Europe and to her past.

This was the reason why the Christian and monastic culture attained in England an independence and autonomy such as it did not possess on the continent except for a time in Spain. In the Frankish dominions the kingdom still kept some of the prestige of the ancient state, and exercised, as we have seen, considerable control over the Church. In England, the Church embodied the whole inheritance of Roman culture as compared with the weak and barbarous tribal states. It was the Church rather than the state that led the way to national unity through its common organisation, its annual synods and its tradition of administration. In the political sphere the Anglo-Saxon culture was singularly barren of achievement. The Northumbrian state fell into weakness and anarchy long before the fall of the Anglian art and culture. The popular conception of the Anglo-Saxon as a kind of mediaeval John Bull is singularly at variance with history. On the material side Anglo-Saxon civilisation was a failure; its chief industry seems to have been the manufacture and export of saints, and even Bede was moved to protest against the excessive multiplication of monastic foundations which seriously weakened the military resources of the state.

But, on the other hand, there has never been an age in which England had a greater influence on continental culture. In art and religion, in scholarship and literature, the Anglo-Saxons of the eighth century were the leaders of their age. At the time when continental civilisation was at its lowest ebb, the conversion of the Anglo-Saxons marked the turn of the tide. The Saxon pilgrims flocked to Rome as the centre of the Christian world and the Papacy found its most devoted allies and servants in the Anglo-Saxon monks and missionaries. The foundations of the new age were laid by the greatest of them all, St. Boniface of Crediton, "the Apostle of Germany," a man who had a deeper influence on the history of Europe than any Englishman who has ever lived. Unlike his Celtic predecessors, he was not an individual missionary, but a statesman and organiser, who was, above all, a servant of the Roman order. To him is due the foundation of the mediaeval German Church and the final conversion of Hesse and Thuringia, the heart of the German land. With the help of his Anglo-Saxon monks and nuns he destroyed the last strong-

holds of Germanic heathenism and planted abbeys and bishoprics on the site of the old Folkburgs and heathen sanctuaries, such as Buraburg, Amoneburg and Fulda. On his return from Rome in 739 he used his authority as Papal Vicar in Germany to reorganise the Bavarian Church and to establish the new dioceses which had so great an importance in German history. For Germany beyond the Rhine was still a land without cities, and the foundation of the new bishoprics meant the creation of new centres of cultural life. It was through the work of St. Boniface that Germany first became a living member of the European society.

This Anglo-Saxon influence is responsible for the first beginnings of vernacular culture in Germany. It is not merely that the Anglo-Saxon missionaries brought with them their custom of providing Latin texts with vernacular glosses, nor even that the earliest monuments of German literature—the old Saxon *Genesis* and the religious epic *Heliand*—seem to derive from the Anglo-Saxon literary tradition. It is that the very idea of a vernacular culture was alien to the traditions of the continental Church and was the characteristic product of the new Christian cultures of Ireland and England, whence it was transmitted to the continent by the missionary movement of the eighth century.

But in addition to this, Boniface was the reformer of the whole Frankish church. The decadent Merovingian dynasty had already given up the substance of its power to the mayors of the palace, but in spite of their military prowess, which saved France from conquest by the Arabs in 735, they had done nothing for culture and had only furthered the degradation of the Frankish Church. Charles Martel had used the abbeys and bishoprics to reward his lay partisans, and had carried out a whole-sale secularisation of Church property. As Boniface wrote to the Pope, "religion is trodden under foot. Benefices are given to greedy laymen or unchaste and publican clerics. All their crimes do not prevent their attaining the priesthood; at last rising in rank as they increase in sin they become bishops, and those of them who can boast that they are not adulterers or fornicators, are drunkards, given up to the chase, and soldiers, who do not shrink from shedding Christian blood." Nevertheless, the successors of Charles Martel, Pepin and Carloman, were favourable to Boniface's reforms. Armed with his special powers as Legate of the Holy See and personal representative of the Pope, he undertook the desecularisation of the Frankish Church.

In a series of great councils held between 742 and 747, he restored the discipline of the Frankish Church and brought it into close relations with the Roman see. It is true that Boniface failed to realise his full programme for the establishment of a regular system of appeals from the local authorities to Rome and for the recognition of the rights of the Papacy in the investure of the bishops. But, though Pepin was unwilling to surrender his control over the Frankish Church, he assisted St. Boniface in the reform of the Church and accepted his ideal of co-operation and harmony between the Frankish state and the Papacy. Henceforward the Carolingian dynasty was to be the patron of the movement of ecclesiastical reform, and found in the Church and the monastic culture and force that it needed for its work of political reorganisation. For it was the Anglo-Saxon monks and above all, St. Boniface who first realised that union of Teutonic initiative and Latin order which is the source of the whole mediaeval development of culture.

No scholar in modern times has contributed more to the study of hagiography than Father HIPPOLYTE DELEHAYE (1859–1941). His bibliography includes more than a thousand books, articles, reviews, and notes. In *The Legends of the Saints,* Father Delehaye shows us the kinds of historically useful information which can be gleaned from hagiographical literature. He is incisively critical of the sources and argues against those who would defend legend at the expense of historical accuracy. Father Delehaye cogently demonstrates that the truth about the saints serves the true faith better than myth and legend.*

Hippolyte Delehaye

How the People Create a Saint

The production of legend is by definition the result of unconscious or unconsidered action working on historical material, the introduction of a subjective element into the realm of fact.

Suppose that on the day after a battle you were to collect eye-witnesses' accounts of it. The engagement would be described in a score of different ways, the same details related from very varying points of view, and all with the same appearance of truthfulness. Each account would be affected by the extent of the narrator's information, his impressions and feelings, the side he was on; his story would be neither wholly true nor wholly false. Each one would tell you his own legend. The combined result of these varying accounts would be a legend too, and if you tried to extract the pure historical truth from it you would have to be satisfied with two or three salient facts that seemed to be established with certainty. Were you to fill in the gaps by a series of deductions, you would be making your own history of the battle, in fact creating a new legend; and you would have to be content with that, or else resign yourself to ignorance.

Everyone realizes the peculiar difficulty of giving an exact account of an event that is too complex to be taken in at a glance. But it does not follow that, these exceptional cases apart, it is quite easy and common to describe something faithfully.

*From Hippolyte Delehaye, *The Legends of the Saints,* translated by Donald Attwater (New York: Fordham University Press, 1962), pp. 12–27. Where foreign-language quotations are given in the text in the original with translations in English in footnotes, the foreign-language quotations have been omitted and the translations placed in the text. Other footnotes have been omitted.

The truth is that in our daily life we are continually taking part in the unconscious process that produces legends; every one of us has had occasion scores of times to notice how difficult it is to recount our observation of something with complete exactness, even if it be only slightly complex.

To begin with, we do not usually grasp a happening in all its details or see the connexion between all its parts; still more rarely do we clearly perceive the causes that are at work, in such a way as to leave no doubt about the motives of the persons concerned. And we instinctively fill the gaps. We reconstruct the continuity of what happened by means of a series of intuitive links, and impose our way of seeing things on the factors that produced this or that result. If we are under the influence of some emotion or opinion that has obscured the clear sight of things, if in our heart we want something that happened not to have happened or not to be known, or that something we did not notice should really have happened, if it suits us that people concerned should have been moved by some particular impulse, why then, almost without thinking about it, we leave one part of the picture in the background or heighten the effect of another part, according to our own requirements. So, unless we strictly control our mental processes and discipline our impressions, we are liable to inject a large subjective element into our account of things, and truth will suffer. To give exact expression to a complex reality calls for sound and practised abilities and considerable effort, and consequently for a stimulus proportioned to the end in view.

It will be agreed that, ordinarily speaking, the average man has not got the mental energy required for this purpose. It is the privilege of only a few to be in the habit of analysing their thoughts and feelings and controlling the least impulses of their hearts, to such a degree that they are always on their guard against that natural tendency to mix up what we imagine with what we know. Even those whose natural gifts and education are well above the average do not invariably bring these advantages into play.

Suppose yourself to have been the eye-witness of a criminal killing. In talking to your friends, you describe the horrifying things that you saw in the smallest detail, nothing about the murderer and his victim seems to have escaped your notice. But then you are called as a witness at the assizes; a man's life depends on your evidence, given under oath. What a difference between the two versions of the same story! Your description is much less clear and full, and has lost the exciting quality you gave to it in private. The reason is that in the serious circumstances of a trial one is much more careful to be exact, and is no longer inclined to give way to the trifling vanity of appearing as a well-informed and interesting person; for the most truthful and honest man may unconsciously start little legends by bringing his own impressions, ideas and feelings into what he reports, thus presenting the truth in a form which, according to the circumstances, is either embellished or distorted.

It need hardly be pointed out that opportunities for error increase in number with the number of intermediaries through whom a story passes. Each one understands it in a certain way and repeats it in his own way. Through not listening properly or through forgetfulness, someone fails to mention an important circumstance and the coherence of the story is thereby impaired. Somebody else, more careful, notices something is missing, and uses his imagination to try and repair the omission; he invents a new detail here, and suppresses another there, till the requirements of likelihood and logic appear to him to be satisfied. This is generally achieved at the expense of truth, the speaker or writer not realizing that he has substituted a quite different story for the primitive version. Sometimes again a story is transmitted through someone who finds it embarrassing, and he contributes seriously to its falsification by some twist of thought or expression.

This sort of thing is happening every day. Whether we are eye-witnesses or intermediaries, our shallow understanding, our carelessness, our emotions and, perhaps above all, our petty prejudices conspire together against the accuracy of a story when we make it our business to repeat one.

This commonplace process becomes much more interesting and fraught with consequences when it takes place on a large scale, when for the understanding and impressions of individuals there are substituted the understanding and impressions of a crowd or of a whole people. These collective and, in a sense, abstract faculties are of a very special kind, their activities governed by laws that have been much studied in recent times as a special department of psychology. The laws that have been formulated were verified by thousands of examples taken from the popular literature of all lands, and hagiographical writings provide a large number that confirm them.

We will not complicate the subject by trying to decide the respective degrees of capacity shown at different social levels. Nothing is more difficult to do, and as regards the matters that concern us here the most diverse elements have to be considered. In the middle ages the whole people were interested in the saints; everybody invoked them, kept their feasts and loved to hear their praises sung. Their legends were developed within a society that was a very mixed one, and it did not lack some persons with certain literary pretensions—I hasten to add that this was of no benefit to the saints.

The intellectual capacity of people at large is manifestly very limited everywhere, and it would be a mistake to suppose that in general it is improved through the influence of the more gifted. On the contrary, it is the *élite* which is acted on by the others, and there would be little logic in attributing special value to a popular tradition because it had grown up in a society that was not without intelligent and able members. In any crowd the better elements are swamped, and the average of intelligence is well below middling; its level can best be gauged by comparing it with the intelligence of a child.

What it comes to is that the generality of human minds can take in only a very few ideas, and those of the simplest. Its deductions are equally simple, made through a few intuitive principles, and they are often no more than mere associations of ideas or images.

The exceeding simplicity of the general mind and disposition is clearly shown in the legends it creates. For instance, the number of people and events it remembers is usually very limited; and its heroes do not live in memory side by side but replace one another, the latest comer inheriting all the qualities and achievements of his predecessors.

Antiquity has bequeathed to us outstanding examples of such "absorption." The wars of many centuries are concentrated beneath the walls of Troy; a prolonged evolution of law-making in Athens and Sparta is put to the credit of Solon and Lycurgus. In later ages it is Alexander, Julius Caesar, Charlemagne who, according to the country, haunt the people's imagination, and honour after honour is heaped on the head of the chosen hero. He it is who was responsible for every striking achievement, the country's welfare and prosperity is due to him, his name is associated with everything noteworthy in the land. Some old legends would have us believe that in all Alexandria there was not a stone that had not been put there by Alexander himself. From the day that Tiberius made Capri the scene of his debaucheries he became as it were the tutelary spirit of the place, whose generous hand has left its mark all over the island.

It is obvious that this habit of concentrating all the glories of the past in a single person seriously alters his real proportions. The glory of his apotheosis is sometimes such that the hero loses his true appearance in it and emerges completely disguised. Virgil, for example, when he became the hero of the Neapolitans, ceased to be the inspired poet and was transformed into the city governor. The local tradition of Sulmona has made Ovid everything that in fact he was not: a skilful wizard, a captain of commerce, a prophet, a preacher, a sort of paladin, yes, and—would you believe it?—a great saint.

Historical truth does not come into the picture, since it is taken for granted of the really popular hero that he is concerned in all important events: the great man has wholly captured the people's imagination, and nothing that is fine, striking or advantageous can happen without his having a hand in it. In the religious sphere, this great man is the saint who is specially revered in the place concerned. Here it is St Martin's name that crops up at every step; there it is St Patrick's. Popular enthusiasm exaggerates the scope of the hero's activities, making it include a mass of things pulled out of their historical setting, or he is credited with achievements of his superseded predecessors.

Above all, it is useless to expect the multitude to distinguish between persons of the same name. Great men are so uncommon! What chance is there that there should be two of the same name? It is reasoning of this kind that has convinced the inhabitants of Calabria that, returning from the First Crusade, St Louis stayed in several of their towns; whereas in fact he never set foot in the neighborhood. The King Louis who marched through the Neapolitan provinces with the remnants of a crusading army was Louis VII. When the holiness of Louis IX had put the renown of all his predecessors in the shade, it was quite natural that he should take the place of the other Louis in people's minds. In the same way did Alexander the Great and Charlemagne absorb all their namesakes.

This shows us that people at large are not, as we are, bothered by chronology. They were not startled to hear it read out, for instance, that St Austremonius was sent to Auvergne by St Clement in the reign of the emperor Decius. It seemed all right to them that there should have been dukes and counts during the same reign; and why should they have suspected that it was an anachronism to give the title of archdeacon to St Stephen and St Lawrence, who were certainly not deacons as that office was understood later?

Neither was geography any difficulty, and distances did not exist. No eyebrow was raised at stories which confused Caesarea Philippi with Caesarea in Palestine, or spoke of a war between the last named city and Carthage. The caravan of seventy camels sent into the desert by the prefect of Périgueux, Isquirinus, to relieve the seventy monks dying of hunger there, did not seem to the hearers any the less interesting because the desert was situated on the banks of the river Dordogne. No doubt they would be more critical about the topography of their own neighborhood, for there the facts were right under their eyes; but why trouble about places that are farther off?

Popular understanding of history is no less unsophisticated. For example, its idea of the persecutions under the Roman empire. No distinction is made between the emperors who ordered or those who allowed proceedings against Christians; there is but one epithet for them, they are all *impiissimus,* whether it be Nero, Decius or Diocletian, Trajan, Marcus Aurelius or Alexander Severus. All are equally inspired by the same insane hatred of Christianity, none has any concern but to destroy it. Often it is the emperor in person who presides at the trial of Christians, involving long journeys for himself which history does not record—and for good reason.

It was obvious that the head of state could not be everywhere at once, but that is no obstacle to his rage; he is worthily represented by emissaries, who scour the whole empire. Christians are outlawed everywhere, searched out and dragged before ferocious judges, who contrive to invent frightful tortures, that in fact were never inflicted on even the worst criminals. The intervention from on high which prevents these ingenious torments from harming the martyrs throws their persecutors' cruelty into higher relief, and at the same time provides an adequate and perceptible explanation of the numerous conversions which atrocious cruelty could do nothing to stop.

That is a miniature sketch of the persecutions as seen in popular legend.

Variations in legislation and in enforcement of the laws, the very marked individuality of the great enemies of Christianity, the local character of some outbreaks in which Christians suffered, such things do not touch the mind of the people at all; they would much rather have a simple picture that is brightly coloured and strongly drawn than a product of all these complicated factors.

Need we add that for them there is no such thing as historical sequence? They do not notice if a martyr's passion is dated indifferently to the reign of the wicked Decius or Numerian or Diocletian. They do not care about the judge's name, and are not puzzled about how the cruel Dacianus could have been at work in both Spain and Italy at the same time. They are not familiar with the long roll of popes, and the part played by a Pope Cyriacus does not arouse suspicion of the legend of the eleven thousand virgins, any more than they are surprised at the mention of a Pope Alexander in that of St Ouen (Audoenus).

Thus historical persons are deprived of their individuality, removed from their proper surroundings, and in a way isolated in time and space, so that their image in people's minds is an incongruous and unreal one. An idealized figure takes the place of history's sharply defined and living portrait, and this figure is no more than the personification of an abstraction: instead of an individual, the people see only a type. Alexander personifies the conqueror; Julius Caesar, the organizational genius of the Roman people; Constantine stands for the Empire regenerated by Christianity.

In truly popular hagiographical legends it is not St Lawrence who is portrayed, but the typical figure of a martyr; later on, St Martin becomes the typical missionary bishop and worker of miracles.

There is the typical persecutor too, Diocletian in particular, and certain judges are as it were incarnations of the cruelty of heathen magistrates. One of the most famous is the formidable Anullinus, who in reality was proconsul of Africa during the great persecution. His name has become a synonym for a slayer of martyrs, and many are the legends that call on him to have Christians put to death, at Lucca, Milan, Ancona, in the days of Nero, Valerian, Gallienus, Maximian, to say nothing of the accounts of what he was really responsible for.

It is not surprising that the reading of some hagiographical documents is a monotonous business, and that there are striking likenesses to be found between the acts of many different martyrs. Historical documents, such as the acts of St Polycarp, of SS. Perpetua and Felicity or of St Cyprian, display notable variations on the one theme; but *legends* of the martyrs are always repeating themselves, for they have almost wholly got rid of the personal element and only an abstract figure is left. Generally speaking, the martyr is everywhere inspired in the same way, voices the same thoughts, undergoes the same ordeals; the holy confessor whose good life has brought him to Heaven must have had all the virtues befitting his state of life, and the hagiographer, faithfully echoing popular tradition, loves to catalogue them.

Look at this protrait of St Fursey: "He was indeed a man of distinguished appearance, chaste in body, single-minded, affable of speech, of attractive presence, endowed with good sense and moderation, of resolute spirit, steadfast in right judgement, constant in long suffering, sturdily patient, quiet and humble, full of charity; and wisdom so adorned the beauty of all his virtues that, as the Apostle wrote, his discourse was at all times gracious, seasoned with salt." That is indeed a fine panegyric; but could not the same be said of every saint?

The biographer of St Aldegund describes her thus: "For her conduct was virtuous, her speech pleasant, she was kind to the poor, she could read easily and give an answer quickly, she was gentle towards everybody, modest among the high-born, like an equal to those below her, and so sparing in her use of food and drink that none of her companions could be compared with her." A few facts illustrating how these virtues were manifested would be far more impressive than this conventional picture. But the people have only a simple, generalized idea of holiness, and the hagiographer is its interpreter. You ask for a living portrait, and he gives you a programme.

What is more, there is very little variety in this programme, for poverty of invention is another characteristic of the popular mind; it always develops along the same lines, and its combinations and permutations show little of interest. The creative faculties seem doomed to barrenness directly people have got a few themes that are sufficient in interest and number to be adaptable to most situations. The comparative study of folk tales has shown that the same stories recur among all peoples and in all lands, that they can be reduced to a small number of subjects that are the same everywhere, and that they appear to have spread over the world from a common stock.

In our day, as we all know, famous sayings are constantly coming out in "new editions" under fresh labels, an amusing anecdote is pinned now on this person, then on that; a classic example is the absent-minded man of legend, whose misfortunes are always the same: what town or village is without a local specimen?

Ancient writers provide any number

of examples of the passing on of legendary themes. We have only to read over the old historians' accounts of well-known military sieges to find that the results of famine, the steadfastness of the besieged, and their tricks to hide their bad state from the enemy are nearly always reported in the same way. When the Gauls laid siege to Rome, soldiers were reduced to soaking leather from their shields and sandals in water to try and extract a little nourishment in this way. If we may believe Livy, the same thing happened at the siege of Casilinum during the second Punic war, and also at the siege of Jerusalem, on the evidence of Josephus. During the same siege of Rome, women cut off their hair to twist it into ropes; the women of Carthage, Salona, Byzantium, Aquileia, Thasos, and yet other cities made this sacrifice too (it may well be called heroic, seeing that contemporary fashion in hairdressing did not require it). Medieval chronicles also are full of ingenious dodges whose aim was to hoodwink the enemy, who are duly taken in and raise the siege. It is sufficient to put these curious stories side by side with others of the same kind to see how much they are worth as history.

Examples could be varied indefinitely, and strange cases adduced of bizarre legends becoming naturalized in the most disparate places. Who would believe that the Irish had thought fit to borrow his donkey's ears from King Midas and to bestow them on at least two of their own kings?

A systematic classification of legendary motifs supplied by hagiographical documents would lead to similar conclusions. Many of the striking episodes that an inexperienced reader takes for original contributions are simply reminiscences, wandering features that have got attached now to one saint, now to another.

The crucifix which miraculously appears to St Hubert between the antlers of a stag is not peculiar to his legend. It is also found in those of St Meinulf and of St Eustace, without speaking of many others wherein differences of detail make the incident less plainly recognizable. Lists have been made of saints who overcame a dragon, but they all need to be made more complete before one could hope to exhaust the subject in some degree. But I do not see any point in doing so. It is nearly always a waste of time to try and find the historical fact which lies behind the introduction of this epic incident into a saint's life: one might just as well ask why a seed carried by the wind has fallen on this spot here rather than that one there.

A critic has rightly expressed distrust of a detail in the acts of SS. Sergius and Bacchus. The body of the second martyr, having been thrown onto the public highway, is protected from marauding dogs by birds of prey. The bodies of St Vincent, St Vitus, St Florian and St Stanislaus of Cracow are protected in the same remarkable way; and we must not forget the eagle which Solomon summoned to guard the body of David, and other parallels in Talmudic writings. Talking of eagles, it is to be remembered that the miraculous bird who spread its wings to shield St Servatius, St Bertulf, St Medard and others from sun and rain is also met in other than hagiographical contexts.

In the Life of St Elizabeth of Hungary we read that her husband, when leaving to go on a crusade, gave her a ring whose stone had the property of breaking when any harm befell the donor. This legend, probably introduced into the story because of some historic happening, is found in a slightly different form in the life of St Honorius of Buzançais. It is a popular feature which has not only been used in the romance of *Flores and Blanche-fleur,* but also in the *Thousand and One Nights,* in a Kalmuk tale and in more than one Indian tale.

The dramatic adventure of St Elizabeth of Portugal's page is a Chirstian adaptation of a story that originated in India; and according to some scholars the story of St Francis Xavier's crucifix, which fell into the sea and was recovered by a crab, is derived from Japanese mythology.

At Valencia in Spain there is kept in Saint Saviour's church an image of Christ which arrived there miraculously by sea, floating against the tide. At Santa Maria del Grao, the port of Valencia, there is another image of Christ, together with the ladder used at his crucifixion; these also came there by sea, in a ship empty alike of crew and freight. The vessel stopped in mid-stream, and the inhabitants on either shore began to quarrel about who should have these holy relics. To settle the dispute, the ship was towed out to the open sea and there set adrift to go where it would; it at once returned to the river and took up its station near the Santa Maria bank.

Pausanias gives a similar account of the coming of the statue of Hercules to Erythrae. It arrived from Tyre on a raft and stopped at the headland of Juno, called Cape Mesata because it is halfway between Erythrae and Khios. As soon as they saw the god, the inhabitants of each town did all they could to ensure possession of it; but the heavens decided in favour of Erythrae. A fisherman from there, named Phormio, was told in a dream that if the women made a tow-rope of their hair they would be able easily to pull the raft; accordingly the Thracian women living in the town sacrificed their locks, and thus won the miraculous statue for Erythrae. The two legends are identical except for the final details.

There is no theme more hackneyed in popular hagiography than the miraculous arrival of the image or the body of a saint in a derelict vessel; nor anything more commonplace than the miraculous stopping of a ship, or the refusal of draught oxen to go on, in order to indicate the place mysteriously predestined to be the home of some sacred treasure or to confirm a church in the lawful ownership of a saint's relics. Think of the arrival of St James in Spain, of St Lubentius at Dietkirchen, of St Maternus at Roden-kirchen, of St Emmeramus at Regensburg, of our Lady's girdle at Prato, of the *Volto Santo* at Lucca.

Research has shown that the miraculous travels of crucifixes, madonnas and images of saints are particularly numerous in Sicily. Similar inquiries elsewhere would probably result in as many discoveries in other countries. In Istria an occurrence of the same kind is associated with Constantine's foundation of the see of Pedena. The panegyrist of St Theodore of Sykeon attributed power of speech to an animal in order to declare the saint's express approval of the resting-place chosen for him. The oxen bringing St Cyril of Gortyna to execution stopped at the right place in consequence of a command from on high, and then there is the part played by camels in the story of St Menas the Egyptian.

There would be no end to a list of the commonplaces of hagiography. The examples we have given show that some of them are very old indeed, and that is a point that cannot be emphasized too much. Many of the legendary motifs found all over the place in the Lives of the saints, in accounts of the foundation of famous shrines and in stories about the origin of some miraculous images, already occur in the classics of antiquity. The ancients themselves would have been hard put to it to tell us where they came from; for them, as for us, they were leaves floating in the air, brought by the wind from afar.

The picture or letter dropped from heaven, the *akheiropoietos* or image not made by human hands, is not an invention of Christian story-tellers. The legend of the Palladium of Troy, the statue of Pallas Athene that fell from the sky and many similar legends show how familiar these ideas were to the men of old. Like ourselves, they knew of sacred images which shed tears, of statues exuding sweat in calamitous times, of voices speaking from marble lips.

The Lives of St Ambrose of Cahors, St Maurilius, St Maglorius, St Kentigern and others tell us of objects lost in the sea and recovered from a fish's belly; it is only a reminiscence of Polycrates' ring, a story known to Herodotus. The bees that swarmed in the cradle of St Ambrose, and also visited St Isidore, had long ago deposited their honey in the mouths of Pindar and of Plato. The rock opening to receive St Thecla and St Ariadne to shelter them from their pursuers is an echo of the fable of Daphne, just as the story of St Barbara recalls that of Danae, whose father shut her up in a brazen tower.

Suetonius relates how, once when he was still a boy, Augustus silenced the frogs that were croaking round his grandfather's country house, and he adds that it is said that since then the frogs there have always been silent. This same marvel has been credited to more than one saint: St Rieul (Regulus) of Senlis, St Antony of Padua, St Benno of Meissen, St George of Suelli, St Ouen, St Harvey (Herveus), St James of the March, St Segnorina, St Ulphia.

It will be remembered with what vigour, at the beginning of his Life of St Paul

[the Hermit], St Jerome describes the horrors of the persecution under Decius and Valerian: the martyr smeared with honey and exposed to the biting of insects, and that other one who bit out his tongue and spat it in the face of a woman sent to seduce him from virtue. The charm and vividness of Jerome's writing give these stories an appearance of authenticity which they can hardly claim. Torture by insects appears to be a reminiscence deriving from Apuleius or some such writer; while the biting out of the tongue was related several times by the ancients, and attributed variously to the Pythagorean Timycha, to the harlot Leaena and to the philosopher Zeno of Elea. In recording this Christian adaptation of an ancient legend, St Jerome did not ensure its final attribution; it was later told of the martyr Nicetas, and Nicephorus Callistus told it yet again, this time of an ascetic who lived in the time of Diocletian.

It is hardly necessary to recall the story of the Seven Sleepers. The theme of a long sleep is already found in the legend of Epimenides, and it has gone on being used in folk tales under numberless forms.

The apparent complexity of certain legends, and the unlooked-for impression made by certain apparently very well contrived arrangements of material, must not deceive us into drawing hasty conclusions in favour of the creative ability of the people's genius. Historical elements which cannot be easily simplified are merely juxtaposed, and held together by threads that are usually of the flimsiest. The resulting narratives are often incoherent and nearly always extremely unconvincing.

But the general effect is not always lacking in grandeur and impressiveness. Here, for instance, is one version of the legend of the wood of Christ's cross. When

Adam was driven from paradise he took with him a branch from the tree of knowledge, and used it as a staff till the end of his days. This staff passed from hand to hand to the patriarchs, and during the wars an angel hid it in a cave, where it was found by Jethro when herding his flocks. In his old age Jethro sent to Moses to come and fetch the staff, which at Moses' approach miraculously sprang towards him. This was the staff on which Moses set up the brazen serpent. Later on it belonged to Phineas, who hid it in a waste place; and at the time of Christ's birth the exact spot was revealed to St Joseph, who recovered the staff at the time of the flight into Egypt. He handed it on to his son Jacob, who in turn gave it to Judas, the betrayer, and from him it came into the hands of Christ's executioners; from it was made the cross on which the Saviour of the world died.

It will be agreed that, reduced to these terms, the legend of the wood of the cross does not display much inventiveness, though the root idea of the underlying continuity of the two Dispensations gives it a certain dignity.

The legend of Judas's thirty pieces of silver has a similar flavour. The coins were minted by Abraham's father, and used by Abraham to buy a piece of land as a burial-place for himself and his family. Later they came into the hands of Jacob's sons, being the money paid them by the slave-dealers to whom they had sold Joseph; Jacob's sons in turn paid the same coins over for the corn that Joseph supplied them with in Egypt. When Jacob died they were expended on spices for his burial, and thus reached the land of Sheba, where they remained till the Queen of Sheba included them amongst other gifts to Solomon's temple. From Jerusalem the coins passed into Arabia to come back again with the Magi.

The Virgin Mary took them with her on the flight into Egypt, and there lost them. They were found by a shepherd who kept them by him until, stricken with leprosy, he went to Jerusalem to ask Christ to cure him. In gratitude he gave the thirty coins to the Temple, and from the hands of the priests they passed to Judas, the wages of his betrayal. When Judas repented and gave back the price of his crime to the priests, they gave half of it to the soldiers who guarded Christ's tomb and the other half to the potter from whom was bought a field wherein to bury strangers.

A similar succession of events has been used to identify the stone in the coronation-chair of the sovereigns of England in Westminster Abbey with the stone used as a pillow by the patriarch Jacob. Many examples could be quoted of such purile linking up of historical memories to produce narratives that appear to be highly elaborated, but which in reality are childishly simple.

The fancies of popular imagination have not been at work only on the famous names and events of sacred history. That imagination has often been given its head with reference to well-known saints, the presence of whose tombs and the existence of a living cultus of whom prevented their being overlooked or confused with one another. The obvious thing to do was to group them together, to contrive family relationships or an activity in common, to invent a story in which each one of them should have his own fixed part to play, without regard to whether the same saint might not be taking incompatible parts in two different groups. Thus whole cycles of legends have arisen that are purely imaginary, in spite of their historical names and a given topographical setting.

The best-known example is that of the

Roman martyrs, whose legends form a series of cycles, each one comprising a number of saints, who frequently had nothing in common but their burial place. Some of these legends are interesting and, in parts, not without poetry; others, and they form the majority, are trifling and irrelevant. All the same, taken as a whole, a picture emerges from these legends, one that was not designed but is nevertheless impressive: if only there had been a poet to work up the raw material of these shapeless stories, the result could have been an epic of Christian Rome from St Peter's foundation of the mother and mistress of the churches, through the bloody conflicts of the days of persecution, down to the victory under Silvester and Constantine. But the genius who might have been able to give us this masterpiece did not appear; and our sense of the subject's grandeur enables us the more to appreciate the poverty of the legends that we have and the lack of inspiration and originality in the productions of the people at large.

Many people envision Charlemagne as the Maker of Europe, the man who developed the institutions upon which the great European monarchies rested. *The Carolingian Empire* by HEINRICH FICHTENAU (b. 1912) is a challenge to this view. Charlemagne and his followers are depicted by Fichtenau in very human terms, and their strengths and weaknesses are explored and examined.*

Heinrich Fichtenau

Charlemagne's Church

Christianity was mostly a matter of theoretical knowledge without any immediate connection with the task of administration; and the pastoral office, like the office of the count, was considered to be essentially a matter of administration. Knowledge of Christianity itself was available only to the few. The majority of priests were not deeply touched by it. Hence it is incorrect to speak, in the age of Charles the Great, of "the Frankish church" as though it were a single unit. The lower clergy, who belonged socially to the servants, to the broad mass of the middle and the lower classes, were quite distinct from the higher clergy, who thought of themselves, with their aristocratic style of life, as part of the *élite*. The life of the lower clergy was not only parallel to, but actually was a part of the life lived by the lay poor.

The pressure exercised by the wealthy landlords upon free-men was experienced also in the ranks of the clergy. It is true that there were priests who "owned" their churches without obligation to any lord and subject only to the official supervision of the bishop of the diocese. Usually they had established themselves on land cleared of forest by the labour of their own hands.

But normally a lord would assign a parish on his estates to one of his serfs, much in the same way as he would assign a cottage to one of his peasants. In such case he not only preserved his own power to dispose of the church but also was

*From Heinrich Fichtenau, *The Carolingian Empire,* translated by Peter Munz (Oxford, Eng.: Basil Blackwell & Mott, Ltd., 1957), pp. 156–176. Footnotes omitted.

reasonably sure that his priest would not make a nuisance of himself with spiritual admonitions. In theory, of course, the land, the buildings and the altar were dedicated to a saint and thus separated from the rest of the lord's domain. But in practice this was not the case. The foundation of a new church might sometimes result in a reorganization within the domain; it might become the centre of a larger area, which was turned into a dependency of the parish. But such reorganization did not separate the new church from the lord's domain, any more than the serf who had been ordained priest by the bishop at the request of his lord, was separated from the rest of the lord's serfs. Very often, however, the proprietary churches themselves were simply dependencies attached to a manor or to the lord's residence—mere adjuncts, like the mill or the stables. In either case, the proprietor could dispose of them freely, in part or in full, and we find the conveyance of relics and of livestock mentioned in the same breath.

To every "proprietary" church there belonged, so to speak, a "proprietary" priest. It was his duty to say mass for his lord on Sunday in the lord's house, to wait upon him at table and to lead the hounds for the hunt. There was hardly anyone of rank in the Frankish kingdom who did not set store on having a "house-priest" of his own, and if the latter were disobedient, he risked corporal punishment, or else was simply dismissed. No class of men, said Agobard of Lyons ten years after Charles's death, are so insecure as priests; they never know how long they will be allowed to keep their church or house. When everyone of substance had his own priest as servant, some particularly ambitious magnates seem even to have tried to revive the practice of aristocratic "proprietary bishops," and it was

necessary to draw attention to an old conciliar decree forbidding the appointment of bishops in small villages and manors.

If the prestige of the *potentes* was increased by possessing the largest number possible of servants, it was their particular delight to emphasize their claim to be above the priesthood. This was due not so much to contempt for the class that was not allowed to wear arms and defend itself, as a desire to assert themselves in relation to the very people who were supposed, in spiritual matters, to be their superiors. It was said that a magnate would go to a bishop and say: "I have a fellow there, a sort of clerk, whom I have brought up and who used to be a serf of mine; maybe I bought him from someone. I want you to ordain him as a priest for me." When such a spiritual serf ran away from his master, it was a legal obligation incumbent on all and sundry to arrest him and to deliver him to his rightful owner. Nobody ever asked why the clerk had run away, although in some cases such an escape was nothing more than a protest against the enforced clerical status.

The law prohibited one lord from appointing another's serf as priest without the latter's permission. But the law never considered the serf's own consent as necessary. In his admonition to the clergy in 811 Charles the Great asked the rhetorical question "where Christ had prescribed, or which of the Apostles had preached, that an ecclesiastical fraternity of canons or monks should be constituted from people who were unwilling and who belonged to a low social order." But even on the royal domain conditions were no better. The *missi* were simply charged to ensure that no more male and female serfs were turned into clerks and nuns than was compatible with the sound administration of the royal domains; they were not to be depleted of labour. Charles discharged his Christian duty by remonstrating with the bishops. He was not really bent upon finding a solution of the conflict between the Germanic and the Christian sense of justice. To ask a serf whether he wanted to become a clerk would have been tantamount to recognizing him as a legal person, to treating him like a free-man. This, in turn, would have entailed a complete revolution in the legal conceptions prevalent among the laity. Canon law, on the other hand, demanded the manumission of the serf before the latter could enter the ranks of the clergy. The lords, however, were not always willing to lose a worker through manumission and to jeopardize their control over the ecclesiastical property with which the priest was invested, by loosening its dependence on themselves. Later on, when Louis the Pious decreed that all priests who were not free were to be removed, the decree remained a dead letter; its enforcement would have interfered too drastically with the whole social system.

It seemed unbecoming for the sons of free-men to belong to an order which numbered so many serfs among its members; the more so as the sons of free-men, upon becoming clerks, were also obliged to renounce their right to bear arms in the army and to sit in the law-courts. We know how much it went against the grain for Charles the Great himself. When a certain Aldrich, a member of the highest aristocracy, with royal blood in his veins, contemplated taking holy orders, he did not hesitate to make attractive offers to restrain the young man from carrying out his plans. Perhaps this story is not to be taken literally, but it is not entirely untrustworthy, and Charles's ideas were shared by Aldrich's family. Indeed, as a result of the conditions described above,

the clerical profession was generally the object of contempt. On the other hand, no matter how much it contradicted the old code of honour of the Frankish upper class, Charles, because of his sense of responsibility for the Christian guidance of his people, gave way to the influence of the church to the extent of officially expressing the desire that many men, free-men as well as the sons of serfs, should be educated for the priesthood. Even in the days of Louis the Pious, however, Thegan tells us of the nobility's widespread contempt for the priesthood. Later this provoked a reaction among the members of the lower clergy which is illustrated by the many anecdotes in which Notker scourges the weaknesses of nobles and *potentes*.

In this sphere, as in so many others, Charles in his legislation endeavoured to create "a peaceful harmony between apparently irreconcilable contradictions," instead of trying to put into practice the rigid distinction between the secular and the ecclesiastical spheres demanded by canon law. Like his predecessors, before him, he opposed specific abuses of the law concerning proprietary churches, but he took no exception to it on principle. Through Charles's intervention the diocesan bishop was at least given a chance of deciding whether a clerk or a priest was entitled "to be so called" and whether he was "blameless." The social and economic conditions of the minor clergy, however, remained unaltered. Only at the end of his reign did Charles try to secure for the bishops the right to some kind of control when lords wished to dismiss their ecclesiastical servants. But it was only under Louis the Pious that the lord's arbitrary power to appoint and depose his clerks was curtailed and that a minimum income was guaranteed as an economic basis for parish services.

The ecclesiastical reform party, however, could not effect more; not even during those years in which the ruler was their willing tool.

The synod of Frankfort of 794 had recognized the right of the magnates to own proprietary churches and had thus confirmed the lord's control over his clerks. In the same spirit the *capitulare de villis* decreed that only such ecclesiastics as belonged to the royal household, in its widest sense, were to be invested with churches on the royal domain. This exclusive rule, which the king and the secular magnates exercised over their churches, was exactly paralleled by that of the major prelates. They too had their "proprietary clergy" of whom they could dispose as a master disposed of a serf, and whom, "acting rather as tyrants than as just rulers," they taxed at rates far above the dues allowed to the ecclesiastical superior by canon law. They were able to do this all the more easily as there existed no permanent authority to supervise them. The secular magnates, if they went too far, were, at least, exposed to episcopal admonitions. But the bishops themselves were free to squeeze money out of their churches until the arrival of the king's *missi*. And even then it was probably not easy to find someone to lay a charge and take the risk of secular as well as of ecclesiastical revenge.

Where ecclesiastical lords confiscated the tithe paid by the faithful and granted it away or sold it, instead of using it for the maintenance of their priests and the upkeep of their churches, the clergy were of necessity prevented from carrying out their appointed tasks and forced to consider other ways of making a living. They not only accepted offices in the administration of the domains of the magnates or in their households; they also engaged in usury and money lending, activities strictly prohibited by the church. "Many work night and day to acquire, through usury, worldly possessions such as chattels, slaves, wine and grain." The capitularies, though full of indignation at such practices, were silent about the conditions that caused them, though these conditions were, of course, no excuse. There must have been many priests who embarked upon shady transactions in times of want and then continued them even when conditions had changed for the better. What drove them on was the desire to make money and to climb socially, which could not be restrained by ecclesiastical prohibitions. "After their ordination, men who previously were poor, buy land and serfs and other property with the money intended for the upkeep of divine service. They achieve nothing either in learning or in collecting books or in performing divine service, but spend their time on banquets, oppression and robbery."

Such was the typical parvenu among the lower clergy. He was numbered among the free-men; possibly he had bought his freedom with the profits from earlier transactions. Owing to lack of supervision by his ecclesiastical superior, he made use of the church property entrusted to his care in order to lord it over others. On many secular estates we find, side by side with a concentration of the lord's rights, developments working in the opposite direction, i.e. a loosening of relationships of dependence and the rise of serfs to the economic status of free-men. In the ecclesiastical sphere developments were analogous. Possession of landed property and serfs, combined with his spiritual authority, enabled a priest to exercise great pressure upon the servile population of his parish. Frequent injunctions against the carrying of arms were directed not only against the higher prelates but also against parish priests of this type. The same was true of the complaint that many ecclesiastics used their spiritual dignity only as a means of collecting together a troop of devoted retainers, and only carried out their ecclesiastical functions in return for payment.

If the conditions in the newly-converted districts of Germany some fifty years earlier are remembered, it will nevertheless be agreed that there had been much improvement by Charles's time. It was certainly bad enough that serfs were forced to become priests. But from the church's point of view, it was better that this should be so than that there should, as Boniface had complained, be no priests at all in many areas. It was easier to put up with priests who failed to commune when saying *mass,* or who gave offence by spitting, than to be confronted, as people had been in 757, with the problem whether sacraments administered by unbaptized priests were valid or not. In spite of the five reforming synods held by St. Boniface, there were at that time clergy who sacrificed animals to the gods, or who lived with five or more concubines simultaneously. In our period the problem was merely whether the clergy ought to be able to read a Latin letter, and how to prevent altogether association with women.

In one sphere only, conditions seem to have improved very slowly since the days of Boniface. It was very difficult to convince the clergy that drunkenness was a vice. The ritual drinking confraternities of heathenism had been given a Christian veneer. They had not died out. Paul the Deacon, a great figure of the Carolingian Renaissance, was the author of a drinking song the verses of which are very reminiscent of ancient oaths. When drinking feasts were held, it was laid down, no priest was to force others to become intoxicated—a deplorable habit which has survived in modern times in clubs and other masculine associations. In those days many a parish priest would drink with his neighbours well into the night and then sleep at the neighbour's house or his own rectory, throughout the following day without holding divine service. When other clergy were present at such gatherings, he would quarrel with them; or even worse, the drinking fellowship *(coniuratio)* would be turned into a conspiracy *(conspiratio)*, directed against their ecclesiastical superiors. It was the same tendency as we have already noted among the laity. The young clerks, living as curates and pupils under the guardianship of the parish priests, naturally behaved in a similar fashion. They cultivated popular songs and games, without disguising them in learned Latin, like the clerks at the royal palace. It was certainly easier for them than for the inmates of nunneries who had to be content with writing out drinking songs and surreptitiously passing them from hand to hand.

Yet there were advantages in the fact that the lesser clergy were not an exclusive order, clearly distinguished from the ordinary people, but had emerged from their ranks and knew how to get along with them. Feasts and popular songs were a medium through which Christian teaching could be brought to circles which had remained close to heathenism. Alcuin himself encouraged a monk—probably in England—to intersperse edifying Christian speeches at drinking parties. When a heathen uprising at the end of the eighth century prevented the Friesian missionary, Liudger, from continuing his activities, he sent out a bard "who was well versed in singing the deeds of the ancients and the battles of the kings," and at the same time was empowered by canon law to perform emergency baptisms. Later on, this Friesian bard also learned to sing psalms, and he probably recited them together with his epics during festivities. All this was in the spirit of the missionary programme which pope Gregory III sent to Boniface: to "propagate the teachings of the Old and the New Testament in a manner adapted to untutored minds."

Since then, it is true, the Frankish clergy had laid more emphasis upon adaptation than upon propagation. They themselves could have done with missionaries; but there was nobody to carry out such work. The only task which the Frankish clergy, on the whole, was able to discharge fully was the administration of the sacraments—although even this was not always performed according to canonical regulations. Even here, however, there were dangers. Time and again we hear complaints that people abandoned their secular status without wishing to become either secular clergy or canons regular or monks. Satisfied with minor orders, they remained mere clerks for the rest of their lives. Many a young curate, whom the parish priest was supposed to educate, saw a more promising career in the service of a lord or even in an unattached life, in which he was not tied to a diocesan bishop, and in the course of which he could find manifold employment as the clerk or official of a noble or as a courtier and councillor to Charles.

Just as the old social order of the Frankish tribe had broken down and given way to fluctuating gradations which no longer corresponded exactly to the old ranks of society, so also an intermediate group gradually grew up between the clergy and the laity. This group was the butt of frequent criticism; but no serious attempt was ever made to exterminate it. We have met its representatives already when discussing the scholars at the Carolingian court. They alone were capable of initiating a reform movement; but they were as little interested in reform as Charles himself, who valued the services of these semi-ecclesiastics so highly. Even so, warning voices were heard during his own life-time. Thus Paul the Deacon wrote that the evil conditions among the clergy were destroying the order of the world; the soil was yielding fewer fruits and the winds were blowing without restraint. This statement adumbrated the future tendency towards a more clear-cut definition of the social hierarchy. Under Louis the Pious the campaign against "the army of the clergy in the palace, popularly known as chaplains," was expressly based upon the contention that these people did not belong to any known ecclesiastical *ordo*. The division into spirituality and laity, and inside the spirituality into monks, canons regular and secular clergy, left no place for the intermediate group that had been responsible for so many excesses as well as for so many positive achievements, particularly in the literary field.

Even the monks did not always stand for that withdrawal from the world and from secular affairs that had been envisaged by the founders of the monastic orders, Benedict and Columban. In Irish monasteries this withdrawal had been effected by a total separation of the monk from his kith and kin. The follower of Christ had been supposed to be a mere wanderer on earth without a fixed abode. But this system had given rise to the first of the spiritual vagrants, who could not be fitted into any local ecclesiastical organization and whose moral discipline no one could supervise. The Irish monks had entered the pagan parts of the continent as wandering pioneers of the church; but this task now seemed to have been accomplished. Already under Pepin the attempt had been made to attach them to a permanent abode by assigning each to a monastery. The Irish "wandering bishops" suffered a similar fate, for their very existence made the creation of a stable ecclesiastical hierarchy difficult. They were turned into "monastic bishops," with the ludicrous result that no less than seven such Irish bishops were congregated together in one monastery in the upper Rhineland in Charles the Great's time.

But the monks' desire to wander was by no means dead. The simplest way of avoiding superior discipline was to go wandering about under the pretext of a pilgrimage, or simply to run away from one's abbot. Or else one tried to found a monastery of one's own in which one could order life according to one's own wishes, gathering together a following of one's own. Indeed, the novice's vows to his abbot followed the formulae of the oath of fealty sworn to a lord, and in the monastery of Reichenau, for example, they were administered by way of personal commendation to the abbot.

All this contradicted the spirit of the monastic rule. In fact, there were religious communities in which sometimes the rules of Benedict of Nursia were obeyed, sometimes the rules for canons regular, and sometimes neither. Not only the official visitor but Charles himself must have been profoundly irritated to find that the "monks" of Tours passed themselves off, as suited them best, for genuine monks, for canons regular or for a mixture of both. Alcuin, as their abbot, should have seen to this. But he himself lived in the no-man's land between the strict monastic rule, the rule for canons which allowed a separate house and income, and the status of a royal chaplain without a fixed abode. As a result he spoke with much sympathy of the "third order" which existed side by side with the monks and canons regular: "They ought not to be despised, for many people of that sort can be found in the house of God."

Already Pepin had decreed, under pain of excommunication, that all who wore the tonsure but had retained their property and lived neither under the disciplinary control of a bishop nor in a monastery, must become either monks or canons regular. But as late as the reign of Charles the Great there were still people who "availed themselves of the monastic habit in order to confuse spiritual with secular business." They drifted about from one urban settlement to another, engaged on the most diverse kinds of business, not always of an honest character. At times, for instance, they travelled in the employment of magnates such as Einhard or archbishop Otger of Mayence, who desired to increase their collection of relics either through purchase or through theft. Some members of the regular clergy, of course, were driven on to the streets by bitter hardship rather than by the desire for profit and freedom. It was well known that there were prelates who withheld from their inferiors their due means of existence, and thus forced them to wander about and engage in dishonest transactions.

Thus the social position of the regular clergy of low birth and without private income was very similar to that of the parish clergy and of the poor among the laity. Side by side with monasteries, such as Corbie, the inmates of which were in large part noblemen, there were monasteries which drew recruits from the male and female serfs of the large domains. A monk might be a poor fellow, a vagrant beggar, or he might be a respected "lord," as was the case in the famous old abbey of Fulda, where land and grain stores had been divided among the monks so that everybody was free to go about his own business. Sometimes, on the other hand, the economic basis of a monastery was too small to support the monks. Vanity and the founder's desire to have people pray for his soul all too often resulted in a poorly endowed new foundation. In such cases, monks were driven to make a living by accepting the office of a bailiff or by concentrating upon trade and usury. Hardship often destroyed the sense of community among the brothers. But even the rich monks of Fulda were wont to quarrel and intrigue with each other about their fields.

If the abbot were a layman, there was probably even less difference between the monastic domain and an ordinary secular estate. On the death of Fardulf, the Lombard who had been granted the abbey of St. Denis as a reward for his betrayal of the conspiracy of the hunch-back Pepin, Waldo of Reichenau had to march with armed men into the chapter-house and force the rebellious monks to fulfil their spiritual duties. Even in monasteries which were in sympathy with reform it was debated whether the house might not fare better under an aristocratic abbot than under a member of the lower orders, no matter how pious the latter might be. "He will defend us against counts and other mighty lords, and his rank will incline even the emperor's favour towards us. Do you know how he can do this? He can do it, because he has relatives in the royal palace." These were, after all, weighty grounds for not departing from accepted custom.

Just as a lord could force a serf against his will to become a secular priest, so also he could force him to take the tonsure of a monk. There were complaints that the victims of such compulsion frequently tended to become criminals and vicious men. This was not always due to the despair felt at being forced into monastic life. On the contrary, dangerous people were often sent to a monastery as a precaution instead of being put under lock and key: aristocratic conspirators, prisoners of war, hostages as well as "evil and ill-disposed men who were capable of any infamous action." It was unlikely that people's respect for the religious profession would be heightened or that monasteries would attract many honourable people, when they had to live there in daily contact with murderers and bloodshedders, and when whole convict colonies, which soon organized themselves into robber confraternities, were settled upon monastic lands.

It certainly suited the secular authorities to rid themselves in this way of opponents or of those involved in a blood feud. In the case of a man involved in a blood feud, however, there was always the danger that the family of the victim would turn their ancient right of revenge against the whole convent. On the other hand, it was equally profitable for an abbot if he could get a premium for accepting novices without probation, or for giving credence to the lies on the pretext of which they were being enticed into the monastery. It could hardly be expected that people who were longing for the secular life of which they had been deprived by such frauds, should turn into models of monasticism. Many such monks tried to drown their sorrows in drink or in even worse ways.

Charles the Great's legislation was confined to denouncing specific consequences of these conditions. No systematic attempt was made to improve monastic discipline as a whole. The responsibility for this rests less in "the Emperor's lukewarm interest" in monasticism than in the fact that any regimentation from above was unlikely to be successful without a corresponding movement for reform among the clergy themselves. Moreover, Charles needed the close support of the aristocracy. Therefore, he always carefully refrained from interfering with the internal administration of both ecclesiastical and secular estates. The condition of the clergy could not, however, be improved without causing, sooner or later, the sharpest conflict over the principles of the proprietary church system, and this would have shattered the established order of the whole realm. At a later date, such an attack was in fact attempted, with singularly little success by the extreme wing of the reformers, under the leadership of bishop Agobard of Lyons.

As far as the spiritual attitude of the Frankish clergy of the period is concerned, it is hardly possible to reduce its varied manifestations to a common denominator. One thing, however, is certain. The real danger did not stem so much from a lack of book learning as from the fact that people were not thoroughly imbued with a Christian spirit. The great missionaries had been men of action, heroic warriors of Christ, just judges of truth and falsehood in the sphere of religion. These ideals may have remained valid for the laity, especially for Charles and the leaders of his armies. But when further conquests became impracticable, the initial spark was soon extinguished. And for the present there was nothing with which to replace it. People did not comprehend—as the Christians of the Orient, nourished by rich sources of spiritual exercise, comprehended—that the time had come to transfer the scene of battle from the world to the soul. Instead, they vainly wasted their energy in external organization. They busied themselves with the administration of

church property, participated in the running of the state, and delivered "thundering" sermons, poor substitutes for the living appeal to the inner man. Men of that age were dependent upon personal example, the place of which could not be taken by books. Perhaps the enormous appeal which the worship of relics made to the people in this time of crisis was due, in part, to the fact that in an age devoid of saints, people desired the bodily presence of the saints of earlier ages.

The religious mood of the people needed saints. When there were none, it created them. There was little reason for worshipping men like Alcuin or Angilbert during their lifetime. But no sooner were they buried than legends began to circulate. They were alleged to have performed miracles, and in the place where they had worked and lived they were considered blessed or were even called saints. Charles, in his legislation, had to oppose the weed-like growth of "false martyrs and unrecognized saints' days." Charles even tried to prohibit altogether the worship of these new saints, whose monuments were being erected at every street corner. The survival of local heathen cults was certainly only a very minor cause of such popular customs; on the contrary the heathen cults and the rise of Frankish Christian local saints, were probably due to the same factor. This was the longing people had to subject themselves, together with their manor or village, to a divine leader or protector, just as in worldly affairs they sought the protection of a "good lord." In seeking a patron saint, people considered themselves, much as in their worldly relationships, as the vassals and followers of a heavenly magnate. This is proved by the willingness with which they were ready to defend his "honour," and the place that was due to him in the heavenly hierarchy. One Sunday, the men of the archbishop of Orléans arrived in St. Martin de Tours to arrest a fugitive who had placed himself under the protection of St. Martin. The peasants, who had been drinking wine in their cottages, rushed out to take up arms: "There is one thing which people of all ages and of all places have in common. They do not suffer their saints to be dishonoured." In return, it was taken for granted that the saint would assist his people in times of want and danger, and this he did by the miracles performed at his grave or when he was invoked. People were proud when it could be shown that their own saint was more powerful than someone else's, to whom pilgrims and the sick had turned in vain.

These things should not be mistaken for a tendency towards polytheism. Just as government formed a graded pyramid between lord and man, which would have been incomplete without its apex—namely, the ruler's dominion over the whole state—so a corresponding order obtained in heaven. Every position, from that of a minor local saint to that of the powerful "prince" who had his own house in the heavenly palace, was strictly graded. The ruler of the universe, Christ-God, whose "honour" was enhanced by the number of his saintly followers and vassals, stood at the summit. A small peasant of Tours could no more address a petition directly to the emperor without first seeking justice from his own abbot, than he could dispense with the intercession of the competent saint. He did not worship St. Martin for the saint's sake but in order to reach, through him, the inner springs of the heavenly kingdom.

The emphasis on the legal order inherent in religion caused men to regulate their conduct, so far as possible, according to the commands of the church and to perform good "works" in large numbers. But, owing to the same legalistic attitude, they rarely embarked upon the struggle for the inner regeneration and sanctification of the individual—a struggle which is as essential for salvation as the performance of good works. Where the inwardness of religion was concerned, the clergy, for the most part, failed to set an example, and in this sphere the saints also were of no avail. They had long since been removed from earthly life and their miraculous intervention, in the form of rewards and punishments, was commonly understood as a sign of their approval or disapproval within the framework of the existing legal system. Popular legends, handed down orally or in writing, offered only slender guidance for self-discipline, for the lives of saints which they recounted were hardly calculated to solve the problems arising in the course of everyday life. Even sacraments were only a very partial help; for people hardly dared to partake of the flesh and blood of the heavenly King; and the remaining sacraments, baptism and confession, were conceived of as legal institutions, primarily concerned with external conduct. The penitential books show clearly how much the Germanic sense of justice was preoccupied with the principle that people were responsible for the results of their actions rather than for their intentions; they never inquire into the inner guilt of a person but always into his actions, which are weighed in terms of unchanging quantitatively assessable penances.

Men judged themselves and others not according to their inner attitudes but according to their overt acts. No law and no sermon, composed on familiar lines, could teach people to lay hold of that inner attitude. The only power able to do so, would have been the constant presence and example of personalities who had achieved their own inner regeneration. The strong but fluid piety of the common people was ready to crystallize around such men. But such men were not available. Hence the Franks sought substitutes by gathering around relics. But relics redirected attention to the sphere of matter and of the senses, and thus turned men away from any preoccupation with the soul, which it was so difficult for ordinary people to comprehend.

Every time a saint was transferred to a new place of worship and every time a church was consecrated, a veritable eruption of popular piety occurred, naively expressed in external actions. "I can neither pass over in silence nor really describe how great was the rejoicing and the pleasure of the crowd who had assembled along the road." Thus reported Einhard, adding that on that occasion even a man engaged in a blood feud had been reconciled with the murderer of his father. When the news that the relics had arrived had spread through Aix-la-Chapelle "everybody abandoned the work in hand and rushed as fast as their legs would carry them to the church." Physical nearness was what people always longed for. In order to enable people to get as close as possible to the tomb of a saint, special circular crypts were constructed, as for instance in the church of the abbey of Werden. Those who could afford to buy relics, carried them in small bags around their necks.

In all these cases an attitude is apparent which is found in old Germanic religion, in which both the sacred and the demonic had been treated as something like a centre from which operative matter radiated. This conception could be applied to human beings as well as to animate and inanimate nature. In the Carolingian age, people still performed sacrifices in honour of the spirits of trees, stones and springs. Bells were baptized in order to render them capable of warding off demonic power. It is true that such practices were waning. The conception that holiness was confined to human beings, even though dead, was gaining ground. And similarly, the idea that evil occurrences were caused by people real or imaginary, was becoming more common. Such explanations of evil occurrences appeared absurd to Agobard of Lyons, but they were at least more rational than earlier beliefs. Thus, for example, people punctually paid fees to weather-wizards who protected them against thunderstorms, while the clergy had to wait for their tithes. In the vicinity of Lyons four people, three men and one woman, about to gather fruit in fields devastated by a gale, had been arrested. It was said that they had fallen down to earth from "airships." They were sentenced to be stoned; but the wrath of the people was directed even more against the people who were alleged to have commissioned them, namely magicians in the country of "Magonia," who were supposed to have sent the aviators and who had planned, after the completion of the expedition, to buy the loot they had collected. Agobard writes with displeasure of this "false belief which has gained such an ascendancy over practically everyone in this region." Similarly, emissaries of the duke of Benevento were held responsible for an epidemic among the cattle. They were alleged to have scattered a poisonous powder on the pastures, and a number of strangers, believed to be the emissaries in question, were captured and forced to confess their guilt. According to the treatment customarily meted out to poisoners, they were tied to boards which were floated down the river until the men were drowned.

Such events show that people were eager to fasten the responsibility for all evil happenings upon actual persons, just as they supposed that saints were the authors of all good things. Just as they conceived the state to be an association of persons, and law to be personal law, so also they thought that natural events were determined by natural or supernatural persons. It was impossible for the clergy who themselves—with rare exceptions, such as Agobard of Lyons —were deeply immersed in popular superstitions, to enlighten them. They merely tried, so far as possible, to prevent people from having dealings with men who boasted of supernatural powers. That this task was taken seriously is shown by the fact that, in the penitential books, those who consulted a soothsayer were subjected to the same penance as people guilty of manslaughter.

Popular imagination was more familiar with sorcerers, soothsayers, witches and other magical powers such as demons in animal shape and haunted places, than with the figure of Satan, their master. The widespread belief in an hierarchical order required that all the demonic powers be subject to a single common head. But the prince of hell always acted through his creatures. He very rarely appeared himself in person. People believed in God but prayed to His saints: they believed in the devil, but protected themselves against his agents. Thus people were relieved in everyday life of the necessity of operating with the difficult, because comprehensive, concepts of "God" and "Devil." It was easier to think in terms of a plurality of single beings each of which had a definite agency for good or evil.

To this relatively peaceful coexistence of saints and sorcerers or goblins in the external world, there corresponded a coexistence of good and evil in the soul of man. In this respect people did not work out consistent attitudes; they lived from occasion to occasion rather than according to the requirements of a single principle. They confessed major sins of commission rather than the attitudes and thoughts that had caused such sins. They even held that a pilgrimage sufficed to cancel all guilt. These attitudes were not due to what, among us moderns, might be called indifference. They were due to the coexistence of a large variety of rules of conduct which had not yet been subjected to a unifying and regulating principle. It might be thought that in so thoroughly religious an age a unification of the principles of conduct ought to have been within the realm of possibilities. Thus, knowledge of God might have become experience of God and gathered, like a magnet, all the scattered elements of piety. Or conversely, people might have realized that behind the threat of total annihilation, there emerged the figure of Antichrist and the Last Judgement.

In fact, such a transformation of the spiritual attitude actually took place. But it occurred not in the reign of Charles the Great but in that of Louis the Pious. Only a relatively small section of his contemporaries were affected, and it was a very gradual process; but the effects of the transformation were nevertheless so great that they not only coloured the outlook of a whole generation but also shook the very foundations of the Carolingian empire. The Christian "radicals" who began this transformation were not sufficiently powerful to put an end to the old conditions; in the end, they were captured by social and political factions and their interests. But, in the first place, their very existence caused a deep rift. The conservatives looked upon the reformers as utopian doctrinaires; while the reformers saw in the conservatives no more than corrupt opportunists.

In the generation after Charles the Great we thus find, separated (as it were) under an X-ray screen, what had appeared earlier as the solid, if not entirely healthy, structure of a single body. It is possible to debate what, in the first place, had caused the separation of the different elements; whether it was the inner stirrings of the monastic reforms inaugurated by Benedict of Aniane, or the increasing poverty and the incompetence of the ruling classes, which led to a more radical type of Christianity. What is certain, however, is that this radicalism would not have had such profound effects upon the structure of the state, unless there had been deep-seated tensions in the structure itself. The age of prosperity was bound to retard the growth of this radicalism; while the increasing poverty of the subsequent years tended to favour it. But sooner or later this radicalism would have manifested itself even without economic causes—for a serious, if ultimately inadequate, attempt to transform a religion (whose external forms had long since been accepted) into a consistent inner attitude, and to mould a way of life that correspond to it, was bound to be made.

The Investiture Contest has been used by historians
to account for Germany's failure to emerge from the
Middle Ages as a unified state. It has also been pointed
to as the catalyst which made the papacy a world power.
In *Church, State, and Christian Society at the Time
of the Investiture Contest,* GERD TELLENBACH
(b. 1903) attempts to understand the movements of
an age, its moods and beliefs. He wishes to provide a
clear picture of what was happening, and, more
importantly, he tries to avoid laying blame or bestowing
praise.*

Gerd Tellenbach

The Church Takes the Offensive

The sixth canon of the Easter synod of
1059 had laid down the programme of
the reformers; its terms—in all probability like their object itself at that time—
were general and unconcrete. With the
march of events, however, the final object
grew larger and nearer, the different
aspects of the dispute were revealed and
became more definite and more readily
apparent. The instructions which went
out from Rome became more definite
and more detailed with every pontificate
after that of Nicholas II. The old reforming decrees, which aimed at a moral
regeneration of the Church, continued,
but in addition to them, and going far
beyond them, there was now the ever-
increasing bias against the laity. As

early as the Easter synod of 1059, Louis
the Pious' statutes defining the rule of
the cathedral clergy were repealed at
Hildebrand's suggestion, on the significant ground that Louis had no power
to alter the true rule without the consent of the Holy See, since, although
emperor by divine right, he was still only
a layman. Under Alexander II, not only
was the canon of 1059 re-enacted, but
there was also a cautious attempt to
limit the royal right of investiture, though
without actually promulgating any new
legislation. Bishop Peter of Florence,
who had requested the king to approve
his election, was sternly rebuked with
the words: "Since no emperor or king
is permitted to meddle with the Church's

*From Gerd Tellenbach, *Church, State, and Christian Society at the Time of the Investiture Contest,*
translated by R. F. Bennett (New York: Humanities Press, Inc., 1959), pp. 112–125. Footnotes omitted.

affairs, it is plain that you did this out of contempt for the Holy See."

Under Nicholas II and Alexander II, and in the early years of Gregory VII, the chief measures taken towards the realization of the programme of 1059 aimed at keeping papal elections free from secular influence and at attempting to secure free canonical election everywhere. According to the new ideas, it was no true election if the bishop was chosen by someone other than the electors and then received the electors' approval; the electors themselves, it was held, must make the choice. Success was at first not very considerable; a hundred years had still to pass before the new conception of canonical election was everywhere understood and accepted. Failure brought about no weakening of the papacy, however; it merely stimulated the angry impetuosity of a Gregory VII. Far from shaking his resolution, defeat only awoke the innate qualities from which he derived the strength and the clearness of thought that made him so great. Had he gained an easy victory, it may be doubted whether Gregory would ever have established the principles on which the position of the papacy and the whole Christian world-order were to be based for centuries.

It was probably at the Easter synod of 1075 that Gregory repeated the prohibition on receiving investiture at the hands of laymen, but in a decisively more concrete form. The king was forbidden to invest with bishoprics or abbacies, and both the person investing and the person invested were threatened with the severest ecclesiastical penalties. This amounted to nothing less than the annulment of the existing ecclesiastical law of the empire. It was an act of unparalleled boldness, more so than even Gregory supposed, and is only to be explained by the fact that he grossly underestimated his chief opponent, Henry IV. His omission to publish the new decree as binding everywhere, and his readiness to accept modifications, were only diplomatic moves, which were abandoned, at any rate as far as Germany was concerned, the moment the inevitable struggle actually broke out. A little later, the prohibition of lay investiture was published with implacable rigour in France by the legate, bishop Hugh of Die. Gregory did, in the event, show himself more moderate than his representative; but if as an act of pure grace he allowed the French bishops who had been deposed for accepting investiture from the king to retain their bishoprics, this none the less clearly emphasised his position. Archbishop Manasses of Reims, the primate of France, who had consecrated a royally-invested bishop, was forced to give way after a struggle lasting many years. The age-old practice of lay investiture was now suddenly to be abolished as "an ancient and very evil custom." After election, consecration, investiture with ring and staff by the metropolitan and enthronement—only after all this should the king give the bishop whatever rights there remained for the crown to confer. Just how much this left to the king was allowed to remain undecided, and did not particularly interest the papalists, so long as it did not adversely affect the freedom of the Church. The reformers of this period were, at any rate, quite convinced that office and endowment formed an indivisible unity like body and soul, and the attempts of the other side to arrive at a compromise, by which only the lands should be conferred by the investiture, met with sharp, even scornful rejection. The sacred character of the lands, as the possession of Christ and the saints, was strongly emphasised; the laity were not permitted to rule them, and any attempt to do so counted as an usurpation of spiritual power.

Lay domination of minor churches was attacked as bitterly as that of bishoprics and abbacies. The old rules governing the dedication of churches were revived; no church was to be dedicated until the founder had set it completely free. The very basis of the proprietary system was called in question when the alienation—even to monasteries—of churches which up till that time had been proprietary, was made dependent on the consent of the diocesan bishop. The council of Clermont proclaimed in 1095 that henceforth it was prohibited for all laymen to retain control of churches, and laymen were even forbidden to have domestic chaplains without the bishop's consent. These were, of course, only theoretical prohibitions; in practice the curia was disposed to be much more conciliatory towards the possession of ordinary churches by laymen than towards their control over bishoprics and abbacies. War had been declared, however, along the whole front.

The Investiture Contest was the first medieval crisis to call forth a considerable propagandist literature, in which the aims of the two parties were reflected. It provided a running commentary on practical politics, and in it the theoretical principles are often formulated more clearly and at greater length than they are in the actions of the great men of the time. The reason for the struggle was everywhere appreciated. Even an opponent of the pope like Wenrich of Trier could write: "That which is done concerning clerical benefices, namely the freeing of them from secular authority, and concerning bishops, who ought not to receive their bishoprics at the hands of a lay prince, all this creates bad blood at first through its very novelty, but there seems none the less to be a certain semblance of justice in it." Lively discussion centred round the part to be assigned to the laity in the Church, and both sides appealed to the authority of canon law. The Investiture Contest gave a definite impulse to the study of canon law. Three important collections of canons were made at Gregory VII's instigation alone—those of cardinals Atto and Deusdedit and that of bishop Anselm of Lucca. The evolution through which the Church had in the meantime passed is well shown by a comparison between the selection made by these canonists from the writings of the Fathers, the decretals of the popes and the decrees of synods, and the selection made by Burchard of Worms at the beginning of the century or even that of the anonymous author of the *Diversorum sententiae patrum*, the "compilation in 74 titles," made in the time of Leo IX. Burchard, though fully conscious of his priestly dignity, in no way criticises lay activity in the Church, and the author of the *Sententiae patrum* is only interested in the primacy of Rome; this, it is true, the Gregorians still emphasised strongly, but they were primarily concerned to provide arguments for the struggle to enforce the withdrawal of the laity.

Urban II continued the work of Gregory VII with skill and greater diplomatic adroitness. If at first the weakness of his position compelled him to exercise self-restraint, his legislation shows no relaxation of the old demands, and he condemns secular control of the Church as vigorously as his great predecessor. In a charter for the bishopric of Maguelonne in the south of France, which had been given to Gregory VII by count Peter of Substantion, we find the words:

"The whole body of Holy Church was endowed, through the mercy of God and the Blood of His only Son, our Saviour, with His own eternal freedom; but through the cunning of evil men and the neglect of the pastors, many churches have fallen into the hands of earthly rulers." As he gained more power, Urban tightened up his legislation against the laity. At the council of Clermont, where he proclaimed the Crusade, he forbade clergy to become the vassals of laymen and to take feudal oaths. It is possible that this had already been discountenanced under Gregory VII; but now, in order to complete the freedom of the Church, it was expressly laid down by law that even that part of the old process of investiture which was based on secular law was to be attacked. The new ordinance was repeatedly re-issued at reforming synods, and Paschal II desired to advance still farther. He made a violent attempt to exclude lay influence from the Church, but took so little account of existing facts that he was bound to fail. His abortive treaty with Henry V, by which the emperor, in return for the surrender of the *regalia,* was to set the Church entirely free, is so well-known that a bare mention of it will suffice.

The object of the so-called Investiture Contest was to drive the laity from the position which several hundred years of royal theocracy and of the proprietary system had given them. There was, however, no thought of attacking proprietary rights as such; so far as they lay in the hands of popes and bishops, monasteries and parish churches, they remained substantially unmolested. We must remember, moreover, that by the eleventh century the majority of *Eigenkirchen*[1] were in fact owned by ecclesias-

---

[1] *Eigenkirchen* are proprietary churches, and an *Eigenkloster* is a proprietary monastery.—Ed.

tical bodies. On the other hand, the reforming spirit did much to promote legislation with the object of reorganising and consolidating the unity of the diocese; and in the course of the next century and a half this legislation was completely successful in grafting private ownership on to the main trunk of the canon law.

This legislation is in no way a discovery of the reforming period, but is simply the old proprietary church legislation specially adapted to the needs of the clerical *Eigenkirchen*. Earlier it had been stated generally that each proprietor must appoint his priest in co-operation with the bishop, to whom the priest would be responsible for the spiritual side of his office. A similar demand was now made on clerical proprietors. If a church is given to a monastery, it was ordered, the priest should remain in possession and receive the same income as before the gift; on his death, the abbot is to seek another and present him to the bishop: if he is suitable, the bishop must accept him; he must be subject to the bishop and pay him the customary dues; he may live with the monks if he so desires: if not, then he is to have as much of the revenues from the endowments of the church as will enable him to live in reasonable comfort and to perform the church services, and the remainder may be applied to the general purposes of the monastery; he is to render account to the bishop for his clerical functions, and to the abbot for the temporalities belonging to the monastery. To some extent, then, the separation of temporalities and spiritualities was recognised in the settlement of the problem of clerical *Eigenkirchen* at a time when it was still being attacked in the case of churches owned by laymen; it prevailed finally in both spheres, and contributed largely towards the transformation of proprietary rights into patronage, both lay and ecclesiastical.

Clerical proprietary rights were not molested, then, but put under the strict control of the appropriate Church official. Many reforming synods even forbade monasteries to acquire churches without the consent of the diocesan bishop. Abbot Frotard of Saint-Pons-de-Thomières, in spite of the fact that he was one of the most outstanding representatives of curial policy in southern France and northern Spain, was deprived of a monastery which he had illegally received from a layman. Devout laymen who wished to make gifts, and the monasteries which were to receive the churches were, however, recommended to seek help from Rome if the bishop refused the necessary permission out of mere avarice. Paschal II seems to have attempted a further step in the limitation of clerical proprietorship, though without success. He wrote to Anselm of Canterbury: "A bishop should not receive churches at the hand of a layman if they lie in a diocese other than his own; in all other cases he may accept them with a clear conscience, for this is no gift, but a restoration. All the churches in the diocese should be in the bishop's power, and abbots should receive them at his hand." Paschal thus wished to prevent bishops possessing *Eigenkirchen* in other bishops' dioceses; had it been possible to carry this measure into effect, the proprietary system would have ceased to act as a force which broke up the unity of the diocese.

The only man whom we know to have contemplated a complete and absolute liberation of the Church from the proprietary system is a Swabian chronicler, supposed to have been Berthold of Reichenau. Recording the Lenten synod of 1078 in his Annals, he writes that anathema was proclaimed not merely against all laymen but even against clerics and all persons who, contrary to the canonical decrees, should give bishoprics, abbacies, priories, churches, tithes or ecclesiastical dignities of any kind to a cleric or any other person as a benefice, if this was done as a result of ancient usurpation. Such a law would have destroyed royal theocracy and the proprietary system at one blow, and this, it seems, is what the chronicler imagined the object of the reformers to be. His description of the legal standing of the monastery of Hirsau is also very remarkable. Hirsau was among the most highly-privileged of the papal *Eigenklöster,* but the Swabian monk, it is plain, intentionally ignored its dependence on the papacy, and regarded it as absolutely free, subject only to the dominion of God and saints Peter, Aurelius and Benedict. Influential leaders of the Church did not draw such conclusions, and indeed would have felt them pointless, for it was only the laity whose rights they wished to limit.

We have seen how this task was ever more clearly perceived, and how the growing consciousness of purpose led to the formulation of more definite demands, which the reformers strove to realize. But the secular powers rapidly collected their forces to resist the onslaught. From the time of William the Conqueror onwards, for instance, the English kings did not allow themselves to be seriously disturbed by the reform programme. Spain was less open to attack, since there the old system was not only deeply rooted, but was used in the Church's interests. In France the king was not in a position to offer serious resistance, but the bishops presented a more difficult problem, and used the revived study of the canon law to find new means of saving many important elements of the existing system. The strongest resistance, however, was met with where the attack had been strongest, in the imperial lands. The last two Salians defended themselves and the foundations of their power against the new ideas with astonishing tactical skill; the retention of control over the German Church was for them a matter of the most urgent political necessity, needing no circumstantial proof, while from the moral point of view, the opponents of the new ideas could comfort themselves with the thought that the existing state of affairs and their existing rights were sanctified by ancient usage.

The power of tradition and the strength of their opponents compelled the leaders of reform to proceed with care, to avoid formulating their principles too bluntly, and occasionally to give way in order to be able to advance elsewhere. It is often difficult to decide whether, in any given case, reform measures had long been planned, but had been held back out of prudence, or whether they arose directly out of the struggle itself. Both suggestions are true; it would be wrong to believe that the reformers already had their programme in their pockets at the accession of Leo IX or at the Easter synod of 1059, and that they proceeded at favourable moments to hold its various points up before an astonished world, but it is certain that political events sometimes promoted and sometimes hindered the cause of reform. The emergence of the fundamental idea of the Gregorian movement in 1058 was caused . . . almost solely by political events. Alexander II, seriously embarrassed by the setting-up of the anti-pope Honorius II, was forced to make concessions and could not proceed so boldly as his predecessor. He, the pope, who was responsible to no man, had to clear himself of the charge of simony before a synod, and to negotiate with the German court about the regularity of his election. It had been no departure from the new principles, on the other hand, when Gregory VII informed the German king that he had been elected, for this announcement was not different in character from that which he sent to other princes, to bishops and to abbots. Yet even Gregory's measures against the laity were sometimes influenced by what were really extraneous incidents. In 1074, for example, he planned a great crusade against the Saracens, intending to bring aid to the Greek empire and so to recover the influence over the Eastern Church which Rome had lost as a result of the schism. When, about the end of the year, he had to drop this plan, he was free to turn to other things, and in the following February he issued the prohibition on lay investitures. Again, the open breach with Henry IV, and the confusion in Germany, by removing any temptation to compromise, led him to pursue his ends with increasing bluntness. The short pontificate of the monastically-inclined Victor III brought a temporary modification into Roman practice, but after his success against the antipope Guibert, Urban II returned to the lines of Gregory's policy and even increased the strictness of the latter's rules; though his crusading plans soon forced him to give way on several points. This is perhaps a sufficient indication of the close connection between the reform movement and the general current of politics.

It is more important to observe in detail that the curia was often driven to abandon principles which had already been proclaimed as canonical, and to determine precisely how much had been attained by the time the struggle ended and how much had had to be given up. A year after the Easter synod of 1059, the cardinal-priest Stephen held a synod in Tours, in which the old legislation favouring the proprietary system was still maintained intact. A synod held at Gerona in 1078 in the presence of Gregory VII's legate, bishop Amatus of Oléron, declared that the laity had, properly speaking, no right to churches; but, recognising that churches could not everywhere be entirely removed from lay ownership, the assembly was content to enact that the laity should at least be prevented from having the offerings. In fact, the ordinary method of procedure was not to deny in principle the right of the laity to own churches, but gradually to annul the rights that flowed from ownership, attempting at the same time by persuasion and threats to move lay owners to a voluntary surrender: Richard of Capua, for example, had to renounce all the churches in his land when he received it in fee from the pope. At the autumn synod of 1078 in Rome, Gregory ordained that the laity should be informed how much they endangered their souls by retaining possession of churches and tithes. Under Urban II a synod laid it down that anyone who possessed a church or its lands by hereditary right should lose his clerical fiefs until he surrendered the church. On the whole, however, the struggle centred round the bishoprics and large abbacies until the concordat of Worms, although the first investiture decrees had not applied to them alone. Even at Calixtus II's general synod at Reims in 1119 a proposed canon had to be significantly altered in deference to stormy protests. In its first form it ran: "We forbid all lay investiture with

churches and clerical estates," but it was modified to read: "We forbid all lay investiture with bishoprics and abbacies;" the prohibition had, in short, to be limited to the higher offices.

The laity did not give up even these, however, without a struggle. When monasteries were voluntarily given to the Holy See, the pope was willing to make concessions to the donors. He might allow them to retain jurisdiction over the lands, or even grant them a share in the choice of the abbot; examples are the concessions made by Nicholas II to viscount Arnald of Ager for San Pedro de Ager, and by Alexander II to the count of Nellenburg for All Saints at Schaffhausen, and Urban II's command that count Bernard of Besalú's consent was to be held necessary to the election of the abbot of San Juan de las Abadesas.

In the same way, the popes were far from insisting rigidly on "canonical election" in strict conformity with the new decrees. It was impossible for them to draw upon themselves the enmity of the whole world, and royal investiture was frequently tolerated both before and after Gregory VII's general prohibition. Alexander II wrote in 1068 to an archbishop of Rouen who had been appointed by William the Conqueror, telling him to accept the election and not attempt to go against what divine providence had ordained for him.

The relations of the curia with England are typical of the way in which the popes had to concentrate their efforts on the most dangerous opponents, and in consequence to modify or even temporarily to abandon their demands in other directions. They refrained at first from attacking royal theocracy and the proprietary system in England, not only because the Conqueror did at least combat simony and priestly marriage with energy, but also because Gregory hoped that the king would hold England from him as a fief, and in consequence did not wish to arouse his antagonism. During the confusion of the period of schism there was the danger of driving William into the camp of Henry IV's antipope, and behind this there was always the risk that England might abandon the papacy altogether. As a result, Rome was prepared to put up with a good deal of laxity. Archbishop Anselm wrote to Paschal II, for instance: "It is sometimes necessary to make certain compromises which depart from apostolic and canonical precept, especially in a kingdom where nearly everything is confused and corrupted, so that very little can be done according to the laws of the Church. I beg for your permission to moderate some things as God shall direct me. I asked the Lord Pope Urban for the same permission, and he put it within my discretion." Paschal granted the request.

The Investiture Contest was settled by compromise in England, France and Germany. The first agreement was reached with France, though no formal treaty was drawn up. There it became the custom for bishops and abbots to be freely elected, and thereupon to request the king's consent, swear the feudal oath to him and be put in possession of the church lands, and finally to receive ordination. The London concordat of 1107 was strongly influenced by the French solution, and set up a similar legal position in England. The concordat of Worms was similar in principle, but its terms were a little more definite; the king obtained only a strictly limited influence over elections, and investiture remained essentially the same, though he was denied the use of the ancient symbols. In Burgundy and Italy, however, he had to be content with far less.

The Church had been compelled to abandon many of its demands, and had been unable entirely to set aside the rights of the laity. No other course had been left to it than to give up the theory — maintained with so much force — of the spiritual character of clerical property and its inseparability from the spiritual office, and to accept the standpoint of its opponents on these matters. In some cases, the Church had been forced to grant the laity a considerable share in elections, and it had failed to win acceptance for its principle that a cleric could not be the feudal vassal of a layman nor swear the feudal oath. The ordinary parish churches and chapels were left entirely outside the scope of the agreements which were drawn up both before and after the turn of the century, and so far as they were concerned success was very modest: laymen long continued to possess churches and monasteries. As a result of all this, it might seem as if the reformed papacy had been defeated and forced to be content with purely formal concessions. But such a conclusion would be false. The main intention had been to deprive the laity of their spiritual functions, and this object had very nearly been attained so far as bishoprics and abbacies were concerned, at least in the agreements made with Germany, France and England. In future, free canonical election made it possible for the Church to choose suitable pastors, and the sacred symbols of spiritual authority, the ring and the staff, were only given at consecration. The lay princes were driven out of the ecclesiastical sphere, and from now on their power was purely secular.

STEVEN RUNCIMAN (b. 1903) is the doyen of living
Crusade historians, and *A History of the Crusades*
is the only large-scale narrative on the subject in
English. Runciman is not only a skilled scholar who
has mastered the remains of a half-dozen medieval
cultures, but also a penetrating analyst of the forces
that were at work in the medieval world.*

Steven Runciman

What Did the Crusades Accomplish?

*"He that increaseth knowledge increaseth
sorrow,"* Ecclesiastes 1, 18

The Crusades were launched to save
Eastern Christendom from the Moslems.
When they ended the whole of Eastern
Christendom was under Moslem rule.
When Pope Urban preached his great
sermon at Clermont the Turks seemed
about to threaten the Bosphorus. When
Pope Pius II preached the last Crusade
the Turks were crossing the Danube.
Of the last fruits of the movement, Rhodes
fell to the Turks in 1523, and Cyprus,
ruined by its wars with Egypt and Genoa
and annexed at last by Venice, passed
to them in 1570. All that was left to the
conquerors from the West was a handful
of Greek islands that Venice continued
precariously to hold. The Turkish advance was checked not by any concerted
effort of Christendom but by the action
of the states most nearly concerned,
Venice and the Hapsburg Empire, with
France, the old protagonist in the Holy
War, persistently supporting the infidel.
The Ottoman Empire began to decline
through its own failure to maintain an
efficient government for its great possessions, till it could no longer oppose
the ambition of its neighbours nor crush
the nationalist spirit of its Christian subjects, preserved by those Churches whose
independence the Crusaders had tried
so hard to destroy.

Seen in the perspective of history the

* From Steven Runciman, *A History of the Crusades,* vol. 3 (London: Cambridge University Press, 1954),
pp. 469–480. Footnotes omitted.

whole Crusading movement was a vast fiasco. The almost miraculous success of the First Crusade set up Frankish states in Outremer; and a century later, when all seemed lost, the gallant effort of the Third Crusade preserved them for another hundred years. But the tenuous kingdom of Jerusalem and its sister principalities were a puny outcome from so much energy and enthusiasm. For three centuries there was hardly a potentate in Europe who did not at some time vow with fervour to go on the Holy War. There was not a country that failed to send soldiers to fight for Christendom in the East. Jerusalem was in the mind of every man and woman. Yet the efforts to hold or to recapture the Holy City were peculiarly capricious and inept. Nor did these efforts have the effect on the general history of the Western Europeans that might have been expected from them. The era of the Crusades is one of the most important in the history of Western civilization. When it began, western Europe was only just emerging from the long period of barbarian invasions that we call the Dark Ages. When it ended, that great burgeoning that we call the Renaissance had just begun. But we cannot assign any direct part in this development to the Crusaders themselves. The Crusades had nothing to do with the new security in the West, which enabled merchants and scholars to travel as they pleased. There was already access to the stored-up learning of the Moslem world through Spain; students, such as Gerbert of Aurillac, had already visited the Spanish centres of education. Throughout the Crusading period itself, it was Sicily rather than the lands of Outremer that provided a meeting-place for Arab, Greek and Western culture. Intellectually, Outremer added next to nothing. It was possible for a man of the calibre of Saint

Louis to spend several years there without the slightest effect on his cultural outlook. If the Emperor Frederick II took an interest in Oriental civilization, that was due to his upbringing in Sicily. Nor did Outremer contribute to the progress of Western art, except in the realm of military architecture and, perhaps, in the introduction of the pointed arch. In the art of warfare, apart from castle-building, the West showed again and again that it learned nothing from the Crusades. The same mistakes were made by every expedition from the First Crusade to the Crusade of Nicopolis. The circumstances of warfare in the East differed so greatly from those in Western Europe that it was only the knights resident in Outremer who troubled to remember past experience. It is possible that the general standard of living in the West was raised by the desire of returning soldiers and pilgrims to copy the comforts of Outremer in their homelands. But the commerce between east and west, though it was increased by the Crusades, did not depend on them for its existence.

It was only in some aspects of the political development of western Europe that the Crusades left a mark. One of Pope Urban's expressed aims in preaching the Crusades was to find some useful work for the turbulent and bellicose barons who otherwise spent their energy on civil wars at home; and the removal of large sections of that unruly element to the East undoubtedly helped the rise of monarchical power in the West, to the ultimate detriment of the Papacy. But meanwhile the Papacy itself benefited. The Pope had launched the Crusade as an international Christian movement under his leadership; and its initial success greatly enhanced his power and prestige. The Crusaders all belonged to his flock. Their conquests were his conquests. As, one by one, the ancient Patriarchates of Antioch, Jerusalem and Constantinople fell under his dominion, it seemed that his claim to be the Head of Christendom was justified. In Church affairs his dominion was vastly extended. Congregations in every part of the Christian world acknowledged his spiritual supremacy. His missionaries travelled as far afield as Ethiopia and China. The whole movement stimulated the organization of the Papal Chancery on a far more international basis than before, and it played a great part in the development of Canon Law. Had the Popes been content to reap ecclesiastical benefits alone, they would have had good cause for self-congratulation. But the times were not yet ready for a clear division between ecclesiastical and lay politics; and in lay politics the Papacy overreached itself. The Crusade commanded respect only when it was directed against the infidel. The Fourth Crusade, directed, if not preached, against the Christians of the East, was followed by a Crusade against the heretics of southern France and the nobles that showed them sympathy; and this was succeeded by Crusades preached against the Hohenstaufen; till at last the Crusade came to mean any war against the enemies of Papal policy, and all the spiritual paraphernalia of indulgences and heavenly rewards was used to support the lay ambitions of the Papal See. The triumph of the Popes in ruining the Emperors both of the East and of the West led them on into the humiliations of the Sicilian war and the captivity at Avignon. The Holy War was warped to become a tragic farce.

Apart from the widening of the spiritual dominion of Rome, the chief benefit obtained by Western Christendom from the Crusades was negative. When they began the main seats of civilization were in the East, at Constantinople and at Cairo. When they ended, civilization had moved its headquarters to Italy and the young countries of the West. The Crusades were not the only cause for the decline of the Moslem world. The invasions of the Turks had already undermined the Abbasid Caliphate of Baghdad and even without the Crusade they might have ultimately brought down the Fatimid Caliphate of Egypt. But had it not been for the incessant irritation of the wars against the Franks, the Turks might well have been integrated into the Arab world and provided for it a new vitality and strength without destroying its basic unity. The Mongol invasions were more destructive still to Arab civilization, and their coming cannot be blamed on the Crusades. But had it not been for the Crusades the Arabs would have been far better able to meet the Mongol aggression. The intrusive Frankish State was a festering sore that the Moslems could never forget. So long as it distracted them they could never wholly concentrate on other problems.

But the real harm done to Islam by the Crusades was subtler. The Islamic State was a theocracy whose political welfare depended on the Caliphate, the line of priest-kings to whom custom had given a hereditary succession. The Crusading attack came when the Abbasid Caliphate was unable politically or geographically to lead Islam against it; and the Fatimid Caliphs, as heretics, could not command a wide enough allegiance. The leaders who arose to defeat the Christians, men like Nur ed-Din and Saladin, were heroic figures who were given respect and devotion, but they were adventurers. The Ayubites, for all their ability, could never be accepted as the supreme rulers of Islam, because they were not Caliphs; they were not even descended from the Prophet. They had no proper place in the theocracy of Islam. The Mongol destruction of Baghdad in some way eased the Moslem task. The Mameluks were able to found a durable state in Egypt because there was no longer a lawful Caliphate in Baghdad, but only a shadowy and spurious line that was kept in honourable confinement in Cairo. The Ottoman Sultans eventually solved the problem by assuming the Caliphate themselves. Their immense power made the Moslem world accept them, but never wholeheartedly; for they too were usurpers and not of the prophet's line. Christianity allowed from the outset a distinction between the things that are Caesar's and the things that are God's; and so, when the medieval conception of the undivided political City of God broke down, its vitality was unimpaired. But Islam was conceived as a political and religious unity. This unity had been cracked before the Crusades; but the events of those centuries made the cracks too wide to be mended. The great Ottoman Sultans achieved a superficial repair, but only for a time. The cracks have endured to this day.

Even more harmful was the effect of the Holy War on the spirit of Islam. Any religion that is based on an exclusive Revelation is bound to show some contempt for the unbeliever. But Islam was not intolerant in its early days. Mahomet himself considered that Jews and Christians had received a partial Revelation and were therefore not to be persecuted. Under the early Caliphs the Christians played an honourable part in Arab society. A remarkably large number of the early Arabic thinkers and writers were Christians, who provided a useful intellectual stimulus; for the Moslems, with their reliance on the Word of God, given once and for all time in the Koran,

tended to remain static and unenterprising in their thought. Nor was the rivalry of the Caliphate with Christian Byzantium entirely unfriendly. Scholars and technicians passed to and fro between the two Empires to their mutual benefit. The Holy War begun by the Franks ruined these good relations. The savage intolerance shown by the Crusaders was answered by growing intolerance amongst the Moslems. The broad humanity of Saladin and his family was soon to be rare amongst their fellow-believers. By the time of the Mameluks, the Moslems were as narrow as the Franks. Their Christian subjects were amongst the first to suffer from it. They never recovered their old easy acquaintanceship with their Moslem neighbours and masters. Their own intellectual life faded away, and with it the widening influence that it had upon Islam. Except in Persia, with its own disquieting heretic traditions, the Moslems enclosed themselves behind the curtain of their faith; and an intolerant faith is incapable of progress.

The harm done by the Crusades to Islam was small in comparison with that done by them to Eastern Christendom. Pope Urban II had bidden the Crusaders go forth that the Christians of the East might be helped and rescued. It was a strange rescue; for when the work was over, Eastern Christendom lay under infidel domination and the Crusaders themselves had done all that they could to prevent its recovery. When they set themselves up in the East they treated their Christian subjects no better than the Caliph had done before them. Indeed, they were sterner, for they interfered in the religious practices of the local churches. When they were ejected they left the local Christians unprotected to bear the wrath of the Moslem conquerors. It is true that the native Christians themselves earned a fuller measure of this wrath by their desperate belief that the Mongols would give them the lasting freedom that they had not obtained from the Franks. Their penalty was severe and complete. Weighed down by cruel restrictions and humiliations they dwindled into unimportance. Even their land was punished. The lovely Syrian coastline was ravaged and left desolate. The Holy City itself sank neglected into a long, untranquil decline.

The tragedy of the Syrian Christians was incidental to the failure of the Crusades; but the destruction of Byzantium was the result of deliberate malice. The real disaster of the Crusades was the inability of Western Christendom to comprehend Byzantium. Throughout the ages there have always been hopeful politicians who believe that if only the peoples of the world could come together they would love and understand each other. It is a tragic delusion. So long as Byzantium and the West had little to do with each other their relations were friendly. Western pilgrims and soldiers of fortune were welcomed in the imperial city and went home to tell of its splendours; but there were not enough of them to make friction. There were occasional bones of contention between the Byzantine Emperor and the Western Powers; but either the bone was dropped in time or some tactful formula for its division was devised. There were constant religious issues, exacerbated by the claims of the Hildebrandine Papacy. But even there, with good-will on both sides, some working arrangement could have been made. But with the Norman determination to expand into the Eastern Mediterranean a new disquieting era began. Byzantine interests were flung into sharp conflict with those of a Western people. The Normans were checked, and the

Crusades were launched as a peace-making move. But there was misunderstanding from the outset. The Emperor thought that it was his Christian duty to restore his frontiers to be a bulwark against the Turks, whom he considered to be the enemy. The Crusaders wished to push on to the Holy Land. They had come to fight the Holy War against the infidels of every race. While their leaders failed to appreciate the Emperor's policy, thousands of soldiers and pilgrims found themselves in a land where the language, the customs and the religion seemed to them strange and incomprehensible and therefore wrong. They expected the peasants and citizens in the territory through which they passed not only to resemble them but also to welcome them. They were doubly disappointed. Quite failing to realize that their thieving and destructive habits could not win them the affection or the respect of their victims, they were hurt, angry and envious. Had it been left to the choice of the ordinary Crusading soldier Constantinople would have been attacked and sacked at a far earlier date. But the leaders of the Crusade were at first too conscious of their Christian duty and restrained their followers. Louis VII refused to accept the advice of some of his nobles and bishops to take arms against the Christian city; and though Frederick Barbarossa toyed with the idea, he controlled his anger and passed by. It was left to the greedy cynics that directed the Fourth Crusade to take advantage of a momentary weakness in the Byzantine state to plot and achieve its destruction.

The Latin Empire of Constantinople, conceived in sin, was a puny child for whose welfare the West eagerly sacrificed the needs of its children in the Holy Land. The Popes themselves were far more anxious to keep the unwilling

Greeks under their ecclesiastical rule than to rescue Jerusalem. When the Byzantines recovered their capital Western pontiffs and politicians alike worked hard to restore Western control. The Crusade had become a movement not for the protection of Christendom but for the establishment of the authority of the Roman Church.

The determination of the Westerners to conquer and colonize the lands of Byzantium was disastrous for the interests of Outremer. It was more disastrous still for European civilization. Constantinople was still the centre of the civilized Christian world. In the pages of Villehardouin we see reflected the impression that it made on the knights that had come from France and Italy to conquer it. They could not believe that so superb a city could exist on earth; it was of all cities the sovereign. Like most barbarian invaders, the men of the Fourth Crusade did not intend to destroy what they found. They meant to share in it and dominate it. But their greed and their clumsiness led them to indulge in irreparable destruction. Only the Venetians, with their higher level of culture, knew what it would be most profitable to save. Italy, indeed, reaped some benefit from the decline and fall of Byzantium. The Frankish settlers in Byzantine lands, though they brought a superficial and romantic vitality to the hills and valleys of Greece, were unfitted to understand the long Greek tradition of culture. But the Italians, whose connections with Greece had never been broken for long, were better able to appreciate the value of what they took; and when the decline of Byzantium meant the dispersal of its scholars, they found a welcome in Italy. The spread of humanism in Italy was an indirect result of the Fourth Crusade.

The Italian Renaissance is a matter of pride for mankind. But it would have been better could it have been achieved without the ruin of Eastern Christendom. Byzantine culture survived the shock of the Fourth Crusade. In the fourteenth and early fifteenth centuries Byzantine art and thought flowered in splendid profusion. But the political basis of the Empire was insecure. Indeed, since 1204 it was no longer an Empire but one state amongst many others as strong or stronger. Faced with the hostility of the West and the rivalry of its Balkan neighbours, it could no longer guard Christendom against the Turks. It was the Crusaders themselves who wilfully broke down the defence of Christendom and thus allowed the infidel to cross the Straits and penetrate into the heart of Europe. The true martyrs of the Crusade were not the gallant knights who fell fighting at the Horns of Hattin or before the towers of Acre, but the innocent Christians of the Balkans, as well as of Anatolia and Syria, who were handed over to persecution and slavery.

To the Crusaders themselves their failures were inexplicable. They were fighting for the cause of the Almighty; and if faith and logic were correct, that cause should have triumphed. In the first flush of success they entitled their chronicles the *Gesta Dei per Francos,* God's work done by the hand of the Franks. But after the First Crusade there followed a long train of disasters; and even the victories of the Third Crusade were incomplete and unsure. There were evil forces about which thwarted God's work. At first the blame could be laid on Byzantium, on the schismatic Emperor and his ungodly people who refused to recognize the divine mission of the Crusaders. But after the Fourth Crusade that excuse could no longer be maintained; yet things went steadily worse. Moralist preachers might claim that God was angry with His warriors because of their sins. There was some truth in this, but as complete explanation it collapsed when Saint Louis led his army into one of the greatest disasters that the Crusaders ever underwent; for Saint Louis was a man whom the medieval world believed to be without sin. In fact it was not so much wickedness as stupidity that ruined the Holy Wars. Yet such is human nature that a man will admit far more readily to being a sinner than a fool. No one amongst the Crusaders would admit that their real crimes were a wilful and narrow ignorance and an irresponsible lack of foresight.

The chief motive that impelled the Christian armies eastward was faith. But the sincerity and simplicity of their faith led them into pitfalls. It carried them through incredible hardships to victory on the First Crusade, whose success seemed miraculous. The Crusaders therefore expected that miracles would continue to save them when difficulties arose. Their confidence made them foolhardy; and even to the end, at Nicopolis as at Antioch, they were certain that they would receive divine support. Again, their faith by its very simplicity made them intolerant. Their God was a jealous God; they could never conceive it possible that the God of Islam might be the same Power. The colonists settled in Outremer might reach a wider view; but the soldiers from the West came to fight for the Christian God; and to them anyone who showed tolerance to the infidel was a traitor. Even those that worshipped the Christian God in a different ritual were suspect and deplored.

This genuine faith was often combined with unashamed greed. Few Christians have ever thought it incongruous to combine God's work with the acquisition of material advantages. That the soldiers of God should extract territory and wealth from the infidel was right. It was justifiable to rob the heretic and the schismatic also. Worldly ambitions helped to produce the gallant adventurousness on which much of the early success of the movement was based. But greed and the lust for power are dangerous masters. They breed impatience; for man's life is short and he needs quick results. They breed jealousy and disloyalty; for offices and possessions are limited, and it is impossible to satisfy every claimant. There was a constant feud between the Franks already established in the East and those that came out to fight the infidel and to seek their fortune. Each saw the war from a different point of view. In the turmoil of envy, distrust and intrigue, few campaigns had much chance of success. Quarrels and inefficiency were enhanced by ignorance. The colonists slowly adapted themselves to the ways and the climate of the Levant; they began to learn how their enemies fought and how to make friends with them. But the newly-come Crusader found himself in an utterly unfamiliar world, and he was usually too proud to admit his limitations. He disliked his cousins of Outremer and would not listen to them. So expedition after expedition made the same mistakes and reached the same sorry end.

Powerful and intelligent leadership might have saved the movement. But the feudal background from which the Crusaders were drawn made it difficult for a leader to be accepted. The Crusades were the Pope's work; but Papal Legates were seldom good generals. There were many able men amongst the Kings of Jerusalem; but they had little authority over their own subjects and none over their visiting allies. The Military Orders, who provided the finest and most experienced soldiers, were independent and jealous of each other. National armies led by a King seemed at one time to offer a better weapon; but though Richard of England, who was a soldier of genius, was one of the few successful commanders amongst the Crusaders, the other royal expeditions were without exception disastrous. It was difficult for any monarch to go campaigning for long in lands so far from his own. Coeur-de-Lion's and Saint Louis's sojourns in the East were made at the expense of the welfare of England and France. The financial cost, in particular, was appallingly high. The Italian cities could make the Crusades a profitable affair; and independent nobles who hoped to found estates or marry heiresses in Outremer might find their outlay returned. But to send the royal army overseas was a costly undertaking with very little hope of material recompense. Special taxes must be raised throughout the kingdom. It was not surprising that practical-minded kings, such as Philip IV of France, preferred to raise the taxes and then stay at home. The ideal leader, a great soldier and diplomat, with time and money to spend in the East and a wide understanding of Eastern ways, was never to be found. It was indeed less remarkable that the Crusading movement faded away in failure than that it should ever have met with success, and that, with scarcely one victory to its credit after its spectacular foundation, Outremer should have lasted for two hundred years.

The triumphs of the Crusade were the triumphs of faith. But faith without wisdom is a dangerous thing. By the inexorable laws of history the whole world pays for the crimes and follies of each of its citizens. In the long sequence of interaction and fusion between Orient and Occident out of which our civilization has grown, the Crusades were a tragic and destructive episode. The historian as he gazes back across the centuries at their gallant story must find his admiration overcast by sorrow at the witness that it bears to the limitations of human nature. There was so much courage and so little honour, so much devotion and so little understanding. High ideals were besmirched by cruelty and greed, enterprise and endurance by a blind and narrow self-righteousness; and the Holy War itself was nothing more than a long act of intolerance in the name of God, which is the sin against the Holy Ghost.

SIDNEY PAINTER (1902–1960) did much to bring to
the scholarly world and to students an awareness of
medieval people as human beings possessed of quite
human strengths and weaknesses. For him the men and
women of medieval Europe were symbols neither of
virtue nor of vice. In *French Chivalry,* Painter discusses
medieval ideas of how the nobility were supposed to
act, and he compares these notions with the far less
romantic reality.*

Sidney Painter

The Knight and the Church

While the conditions of life in their
natural habitat, the feudal court and the
field of battle, were encouraging the
nobles of France to develop . . . ethical
ideas . . . , two alien environments, the
cloister and the bedroom, were forcing
other points of view on their attention.
Churchmen and ladies were creating and
propagating their own distinct and rather
contradictory conceptions of the perfect
nobleman. The first of these, the chivalric
ideas propounded by ecclesiastics, will
be the subject of this chapter. Since one
of the chief functions of the church was
to teach the Christian mode of life, there
had, of course, been no time since the
evangelization of the Teutonic barbarians
when the clergy was not attempting to
modify the ethical ideas and practices
of the warriors of western Europe. They
had tried to confine the robust lust of
the Frankish aristocrats within the bounds
of permanent monogamic marriage and
had sought to curb their pride, avarice,
and gluttony. Even more important from
the point of view of society were the
church's persistent efforts to reduce the
aristocratic propensity to homicide and
rapine or at least to mitigate its results.
Although as early as the time of St. Augustine the church had modified its
original abhorrence of all homicide to
permit the killing of enemies and the
execution of criminals at the command
of a duly constituted authority, it stead-
fastly opposed the indiscriminate violence
which marked the ninth and tenth centuries. The direct line of attack on this

*From Sidney Painter, *French Chivalry* (Baltimore: The Johns Hopkins Press, 1940), pp. 65–94. Footnotes omitted.

evil, the attempt to persuade an aristocracy whose chief function was fighting that homicide should be abjured, was naturally not very fruitful, but the church made some progress in its efforts to mitigate the horrors of feudal warfare. The "Truce and Peace of God" forbade war on certain days and protected noncombatants such as clergy, women, merchants, and peasants. These edicts had some beneficial effect even when they were enforced only by the spiritual power of the church, and they furnished excellent programs for feudal princes like William the Conqueror who wished to establish order in their domains. Then too by preaching the spiritual rewards that would be granted to those who fought the enemies of Christ the clergy moved many an eleventh-century noble to turn his martial energies against the Moslems who held Spain. In short from the sixth to the eleventh centuries the church strove to curb the typical vices of the warrior class or turn them into channels it approved. But during this period the exhortations of the clergy were addressed to the nobles as Christians who were bound as were all men to obey the laws of Christ. There was no suggestion that because a man was a noble he owed special obligations to the church and society. It was the appearance of this conception which seems to me to mark the beginning of religious chivalry. As long as the church simply maintained that a vicious noble was not a true Christian, its efforts and their results lie in the field of the historian of morals in general. Only when the clergy began to preach that a noble who violated certain rules was no true knight did its ideas come within the proper scope of the student of chivalry.

The earliest clear indication that I can find of the existence of this idea that a knight was peculiarly bound to obey and serve the church appears in the contemporary reports of the famous sermon with which in 1095 Pope Urban II roused the chivalry of Europe to undertake the First Crusade. While several of these reports definitely suggest this new conception of knighthood, a phrase in one of them expresses it unmistakably. "Now they may become knights who hitherto existed as robbers." In other words the nobles who ignored the church's injunction to abstain from rapine were not knights. During the next fifty years after Urban's speech at Clermont-Ferrand I can find only two unequivocal references to this idea. Suger, abbot of St. Denis, while speaking of the notorious noble brigand Thomas de Marly states that a church council declared him unworthy to wear the belt of a knight. William of St. Thierry, friend and biographer of Bernard of Clairvaux, in describing St. Bernard's father calls him a man of "ancient and legitimate chivalry." He made war according to the rules laid down by the church and abstained from plundering. In this half century after the First Crusade the chief expounder of the duties of knights toward the church was, of course, Bernard himself, but his remarks on the subject were addressed to the Templars. As the Templars were a military monastic order, in Bernard's own words both knights and monks, his injunctions to them cannot be taken as an expression of his views on the duties and obligations of knights in general. Hence the famous *De laude novae militiae* is of little use to the historian of chivalry. In fact the employment of the word *novae* clearly implies that Bernard had no intention of restricting the term knight to those who followed his precepts. Thus the first half of the twelfth century furnishes little material to our purpose. It was not until after 1150 that ecclesiastical writers began to expound their views on the proper relations of knights to the church in extended and orderly form.

The most distinguished and probably the earliest of these mid-twelfth-century writers was the noted scholar John of Salisbury. In the sixth book of his *Policraticus* John presents a scathing criticism of the knights of his day and expounds his views on the qualities knights should possess and their proper function in society. As the minds of mediaeval men and particularly mediaeval churchmen were deeply imbued with the sanctity of custom and tradition, John felt called upon to produce authority and precedent for his conception of knighthood. He did this by making the twelfth-century *miles* or knight the successor to the Roman *miles* or legionary. The Roman legionary was a picked man, highly trained and rigidly disciplined, who was bound by a special oath to the service of the prince and the state. Hence men who were to be made knights should be carefully selected for soundness of blood, vigor of body, and courage of heart. Before receiving their belt of knighthood, they should take the "soldier's oath" to serve their prince loyally. As no one could serve a prince loyally who did not obey God and the church, this obligation was implied in the oath. These chosen and oath-bound men should then be rigorously trained in military science and bodily exercise. They should eschew luxury and display — should be temperate and chaste. Courage, hardihood, and knowledge of strategy and the use of arms should be their characteristics. If they failed to observe their oath or if they proved cowardly and incompetent, they should be deprived of their knightly belts and severely punished. The social function of knights is described by John with complete clarity.

But what is the office of the duly ordained soldiery? To defend the church, to assail infidelity, to venerate the priesthood, to protect the poor from injuries, to pacify the province, to pour out their blood for their brothers (as the formula of their oath instructs them), and, if need be, to lay down their lives. The high praises of God are in their throat, and two-edged swords are in their hands to execute punishment on the nations and rebuke upon the peoples, and to bind their kings in chains and their nobles in links of iron. But to what end? To the end that they may serve madness, vanity, avarice, or their own private self-will? By no means. Rather to the end that they may execute the judgment that is committed to them to execute; wherein each follows not his own will but the deliberate decision of God, the angels, and men, in accordance with equity and the public utility.

Despite the somewhat puzzling quotation from the psalms the general purport of this statement is clear. The knight should be a policeman bound to execute the orders of church and state. Such in brief was John of Salisbury's theory of chivalry. Some aspects of his ideas require separate discussion.

John, of course, was fully aware that the term knight in his day did not mean any specially selected man who had taken a distinctive oath but simply an adult noble who possessed complete military equipment. He solved this difficulty as had Pope Urban. At the end of his fiery denunciation of contemporary knights he said "For it is nothing to the point if the men I have been speaking of walk crookedly, for such men are not under military law because, if we speak accurately, none of them is a true soldier." In short only those who followed his precepts were true knights. The coward, the brigand, the plunderer of churches, the oppressor of the poor, the glutton, and the debauché were false knights who should be deprived of the insignia of their rank. Although John clearly has the conception of the "order of knighthood"—an oath-bound brotherhood of chosen men possessing certain qualities and admitting certain obligations—he does not state this theory as definitely as later writers. Still the implication is unmistakable. The military profession was instituted by God. Priests and knights are compared. "The former are called by the tongue of the pontiff to the service of the altar and the care of the church. The latter are chosen for the defence of the commonwealth by the tongue of the leader." The two divinely instituted orders which play so important a part in chivalric literature are here in embryo. While this idea undoubtedly sprang from the well-known threefold division of mankind into fighters, prayers, and workers, it is not quite the same thing. John's clergy and knights are selected, consecrated groups, not mere subdivisions of humanity.

Naturally John of Salisbury's chief interest lay in emphasizing the obligations of knights toward the church. "This rule must be enjoined upon and fulfilled by every soldier, namely, that he shall keep inviolate the faith which he owes first to God and afterwards to the prince and the commonwealth." John could not understand how any prince could trust a man who was unfaithful to his obligations to God and His church. He was also anxious to encourage the inclusion of some form of religious ceremony among those by which a man was made a knight. He spoke with approval of a custom by which a candidate for knighthood offered his sword to God on the altar of a church. While John referred to this usage as if it were a generally accepted practice in his day, we have ample evidence to show that it was by no means universal. John was simply encouraging what he

considered a wholesome custom. He conceived of the knight as the special servant of church and prince and felt that the ceremonies by which he was inducted into office should reflect both obligations.

The *Policraticus* contains all the essential features of religious chivalry. Later writers expanded the ideas and developed them in greater detail, but the general picture remained unchanged. A true knight must be courageous, hardy, and skilled in the use of arms, for fighting was his function in life. He must obey the commands of the church and use his sword in its defense. Finally he must serve his prince in defending the state and punishing criminals. His was the might that would enforce the laws of church and state. As John of Salisbury wrote in solemn scholarly latin, his words cannot be considered as direct propaganda addressed to knights. He was laying down a program for his ecclesiastical contemporaries, and it soon found expression in vernacular writings and popular sermons. One can hardly conceive of anyone reading the *Policraticus* aloud in a castle hall, but Stephen of Fougères' *Livre des manières* might well have entertained a reasonably serious-minded baron.

Stephen of Fougères had been, as had John of Salisbury, a clerk attached to the court of King Henry II of England and through that monarch's patronage had become bishop of Rennes. Some scholars have maintained that he read the *Policraticus* and drew from it many of his ideas, but this seems far from certain. One can merely say that he was a contemporary and very possibly an acquaintance of John of Salisbury and that both men used the same general fund of ideas. Stephen's *Livre des manières* consists of a diatribe against the ways of his time interspersed with moral advice. His views on chivalry were very similar to John's though expressed rather more definitely. A free man, born of a free mother, who had received the order of knighthood was bound to be effective in battle, brave, honest, loyal, and devoted to the church. He should not deny the church its tithes nor attempt to infeudate them. Unworthy knights should be deprived of their swords, have their spurs cut off, and be driven from the order. It should be noticed that Stephen emphasizes noble blood as a prerequisite for knighthood far more clearly than did John of Salisbury. Although John stated that knights should be of good family because such men were less likely to be cowards, his main interest was in their physical and mental fitness. Stephen assumed that a knight was a noble, free man born of a free mother. Like John he insisted on the knights' obligations to the church and wished to deprive the unworthy of their rank. He definitely stated what John had merely suggested—that knights formed an order similar to that of the clergy. There were two swords, the spiritual and the temporal. The former had been given to clerks to excommunicate the wicked; the latter had been given to knights so that they might cut off the feet or hands of malefactors. The good of society demanded the cooperation of these two orders in wielding their swords against evil. Thus in this simple vernacular poem we have the ecclesiastical conception of chivalry expressed in a form that knights could comprehend.

While the *Livre des manières* was written in a language and form that knights could understand, it seems unlikely that many nobles ever heard of it. Few knights could read, and despite its vigorous and pungent style this work can hardly have formed a part of the repertoire of wander-

ing minstrels. For the successful propagation of their chivalric ideas the clergy were forced to seek other media. Probably the most effective course was to insert their teachings in songs and romances. At the very beginning of the twelfth century before ecclesiastical chivalry had assumed definite form under the hands of St. Bernard and John of Salisbury many of its ideas appeared in the *Chanson de Roland.* Even if one does not accept M. Bédier's implication that this song was essentially a piece of advertising to attract pilgrims to the monasteries and shrines which lined the road to the tomb of St. James at Compostella, it is clear that most of the material for its composition was gathered from religious houses along that great pilgrimage route. In the second half of the twelfth century the piety of old age and a religiously minded patron moved Chrétien de Troyes to produce *Perceval.* The creator of Galahad, the author of the *Queste del Saint Graal,* was almost certainly a Cistercian monk.

The *Chanson de Roland* is based on the conception of loyal service to God and the emperor. Roland followed his liege lord against the enemies of Christ and as he died he extended his right gauntlet toward the sky in token of his vassalage to God. War against the infidel was one of the chief themes of the *chansons de geste.* Perceval and Galahad represent ecclesiastical chivalry expressed in terms of Arthurian romance. The latter divided his time about equally between performing heroic knightly deeds, resisting the advances of luscious ladies, and listening to moral discourses in monastic cloisters. In the earlier stories of the Arthurian cycle the knights roamed the world for the love of their ladies or in search of martial glory. The invention of the quest of the Holy Grail supplied a religious purpose for their activities. It would obviously be utterly reckless to state that Roland, Guillaume d'Orange, Perceval, Galahad, and the quest of the Holy Grail were invented in order to instill the ideas of religious chivalry in the nobles of France. One could argue equally plausibly that their existence in literature showed that these ideas were already popular among the knights and ladies for whom the stories were written. We can merely say that by finding their way into literature they forced themselves on the attention of the noble class.

One of the chief methods by which the church impressed its views on the laity was through sermons, and this medium was not neglected by the proponents of religious chivalry. Late in the twelfth or early in the thirteenth century Master Alan of Lille, perhaps the most celebrated scholar of his day, composed a short handbook for preachers. Among many model sermons he included one particularly addressed to knights. "For this purpose have knights been specially instituted—that they may defend their fatherland and ward off from the church the injuries of violent men. . . . They prostitute their knighthood who fight for profit. Those who take arms so that they may plunder are not knights but robbers and plunderers, not defenders but invaders." It is, of course, impossible to say how often such sermons were actually preached, but it seems safe to assume that at least once in his life a knight would hear the religious conception of chivalry propounded from the pulpit.

So far this chapter has consisted of a discussion of various ideas which churchmen of the eleventh and twelfth centuries were trying to instill in the minds of the nobles of France. There has been no attempt to describe a perfect knight according to the doctrines of religious chivalry, and this task would be essentially impossible. Except for St. Bernard whose words are inapplicable because they were addressed to the Templars no writer furnishes a complete picture of the ideal knight from a purely ecclesiastical point of view. The closest approach to such a work is *Le libre del orde de cauayleria* written by the Catalan Ramon Lull towards the end of the thirteenth century. After passing his youth at the court of the king of Aragon, Lull turned religious and devoted the remainder of his life to schemes for winning the Moslems to Christianity through missionary efforts. When he wrote his book on knighthood, Lull was a clergyman, but the fact that he had lived for years as a lay gentleman influenced his views. Although in general his conception of chivalry is in accord with that of the church, his opinions would have not received the full approval of John of Salisbury or Alan of Lille. For instance John in common with most churchmen abhorred tournaments, but Lull considers them a necessary part of a knight's activities. John frowned on worldly glory as a motive for knightly deeds, while Lull speaks of it as the only proper one for a true knight. The former writes from the point of view of the church alone, the latter from that of the knight as well. Hence Lull's conception of chivalry is really a combination of the feudal and religious. Nevertheless his emphasis on the ideas propounded by the church seems to justify the discussion of his work in a chapter devoted to religious chivalry. There is no conclusive evidence as to how popular Lull's book was in his own day, but by the fifteenth century it had become the standard handbook of chivalry. Originally written in Catalan it was translated into French by various writers who did not scruple to modify and add to their original. Caxton translated and printed one of these French versions while Sir Gilbert de la Haye rendered another into Scots. Caxton presented his edition to King Richard III and suggested that the king "command this book to be had and read unto other young lords knights and gentlemen within this realm that the noble order of chivalry be hereafter better used and honored than it has been in late days passed." Caxton could not revive chivalry, but he did place Lull's work in a dominant position among the sources used by later English writers on the subject.

Lull's ideas about chivalry can be arranged for convenience in discussion under four general headings—the origin and nature of the order, its function, the qualities proper to a knight, and the education of aspirants to knighthood. As was becoming in one who wished to make a complete and orderly presentation of his subject Lull began his discourse on chivalry with an account of the origin of the order. In an age which traced the descent of both French and English from the exiled Trojans this description of the inception of chivalry was bound to be purely mythical: at a time when virtue had disappeared and vice reigned on earth God divided all men into thousands and in each group chose the most loyal, strongest, bravest, and best educated man to be a knight. Having supplied an exalted origin for chivalry Lull went on to discuss the nature and position of the order. Here the author's knightly background decidedly influenced his ideas. The dignity of the order of chivalry was so great that it was not enough that its members be chosen men equipped with the best of arms but they should enjoy eminent worldly rank as well. A knight should be lord over many men and should

have a squire to care for him and his mount. The common people should work to support the knight so that he might live in complete economic security and pass his time in hunting and martial exercise. Ideally every knight ought to be master of a large territory and its inhabitants. Unfortunately there were too many knights, and only a few of them could be kings or great barons. Hence all temporal princes should choose only knights as their officers so that as many as possible of the order could enjoy the dignity to which they were entitled. Lull was forced to admit that knights lacked the education required of a judge, but they were pre-eminently fitted for all other offices. This is a fascinating piece of knightly propaganda! Lull in common with the nobles of his day resented the inclination of the feudal princes to fill their administrative offices with obedient and tractable townsmen. In order to heighten still further the dignity of the order Lull followed the tradition of comparing chivalry and clergy. Knights and clerks held the two most honorable offices in the world and should cooperate with each other in every way. As God instituted both orders, no member of either one was justified in attacking the other. The clergy urge the common people to virtue by learning and example, while the knights accomplish the same end by the terror inspired by their swords. In short Lull maintained that the members of the divinely instituted order of chivalry should be rich and powerful nobles who combined with the clergy to enforce God's will.

The function of the chivalric order was to supply the force needed to maintain the laws of God and man. The common people labored and cultivated the earth because of their terror of the knights. The same dread made them obey the laws of church and state. The knight's first duty was to maintain and defend the Holy Catholic Faith and the church that nurtured it. His second was to maintain and defend his earthly lord and his native land. His devotion to the church should lead him to protect its special charges—women, widows, orphans, and all the weak and helpless. His obligations to his lord and country included not only their defense against foreign foes but also the suppression of robbers and criminals of all kinds. In order to keep in condition to perform his duties a knight should devote himself to martial exercise and noble sports. He should joust, tourney, and hunt wild beasts. Once more Lull's youth had its say. The obligations of his ideal knight were those envisaged by John of Salisbury and other ecclesiastical writers, but his exercises and diversions were those of the extremely imperfect nobles of the day. Lull could not counsel knights to abandon chase and joust.

The qualities which Lull considered requisite for a knight were a combination of martial and Christian virtues. The former were, of course, absolutely necessary. A knight had to be brave, strong of body, and skilled in the use of arms. Lull did suggest, however, that bravery was more effective when combined with intelligence. Then the knight should be courteous to all, keep himself well armed and well dressed, and maintain a suitable retinue. He should abjure perjury and lies, should be humble and chaste. Finally toward the end of his work Lull listed the Christian virtues and vices and showed how the former were necessary to and the latter destructive of a true knight. But martial and spiritual qualities were not enough for Lull's perfect knight. While he admitted that it was possible for new knightly lines to be founded by

exceptional men, he emphasized the importance of noble birth. His translators dropped the qualification and enlarged on the rule. Beauty or at least normality of physique was another qualification—one who was lame, too fat, or in any way deformed should never be made a knight. Furthermore the knight had to be rich enough to maintain himself in the way of life proper to his place in society. Most important of all a true knight had to be actuated by a spirit of dedication. If he sought solely his own profit and honor rather than the reputation of the order as a whole, he was not fit to be a knight.

A large part of *Le libre del orde de cauayleria* is devoted to a discussion of the training of aspirants to knighthood and the ceremonies which should attend their reception into the order. As these questions concern the means of achieving the chivalric ideal rather than the ideas of chivalry, they are not entirely germane to my subject, but they are too interesting to be passed over. Lull expressed dissatisfaction with the contemporary method of training young nobles. The son of a knight was placed in a noble household where he acquired his knightly education while serving as page and squire. Lull criticized this eminently practical apprentice system not for inefficiency but for lack of dignity. Other professions, such as the religious, law, and medicine, were learned from books, and the military was entitled to equal consideration. He wanted the knowledge that was requisite for a knight reduced to writing so that aspirants could study it in schools of chivalry. On the basis of these statements Lull has been charged with expressing the utterly silly idea that skill in arms could be learned from books, but this does not seem justified. He did not want to abolish the period of apprenticeship. He merely wished to add to it some formal study in books. Furthermore it is clear from the early part of *Le libre del orde de cauayleria* that he considered this work a suitable textbook for young nobles who aspired to be knights. He did not conceive of having squires read books on the care of horses—such things they would learn by practice. It was the history of the chivalric order, its proper function in society, and the ethical principles which governed true knights that he wished the squires to study. In short Lull was partly the author encouraging the reading of his book and partly the enthusiast seeking to propagate an ideal. After his term of service as page and squire Lull wished the young noble to attend a school of chivalry where he would learn the duties and qualities of a true knight by reading *Le libre del orde de cauayleria*.

The chief interest in Lull's description of the ceremonies which should be performed when a man was made a knight lies in the prominent part given to the church. John of Salisbury and Stephen of Fougères had wished to have the aspirant to knighthood offer his sword on an altar as a token of his obligations to God and the church. Lull adds so many religious observances that the whole ceremony becomes decidedly ecclesiastical. On the day before he was to be dubbed a knight the young noble confessed. That night he passed in the church fasting and praying. In the morning he attended mass and listened to a sermon. The actual dubbing was performed while the squire knelt before the altar. The knight who was receiving him into the order girded on the novice's sword, kissed him, and gave him the ceremonial blow. Then the new knight rode through the town so that all could see him. That same day he

gave a great feast for everyone who had attended the ceremony. Finally he and the knight who had dubbed him exchanged gifts and the heralds were duly fed. Again one seems to see Lull in a dual role. The solemn missionary to the Moslems described the formal ceremonies, but the gay young Catalan courtier planned the closing festivities.

One more aspect of Lull's book is worthy of mention—his discussion of the symbolical significance of the various articles which made up the equipment of a knight. The men of the Middle Ages were devoted to symbolism, but nowhere did this taste flourish more magnificently than among the ecclesiastical writers on chivalry. Every article of knightly equipment, even every part of an article, had its significance. True, no two writers were likely to attach the same meaning to an article, but this merely gave freer rein to the creative imagination. One of the earliest complete systems of symbolism for knightly arms was produced by Robert of Blois in his *Enseignement des princes*. A few examples must suffice. The sword is clear and well polished— the knight should be honest and straight. The shield represents charity which covers many sins. The lance which pierces the foe before he gets near symbolizes foresight. Lull began his discussion of this subject by pointing out that every article of priestly vestments had its symbolic significance. Hence as knights were an order similar to the clergy, their equipment should also have a meaning. The sword is shaped like a cross. This signifies that knights should use the sword to slay foes of the cross. The sword has two edges to remind the knight that he should defend chivalry and justice. The shield symbolizes the office of a knight. As a knight places his shield between himself and his enemy, so a knight stands between prince and people. The knight should receive the blows aimed at his lord as his shield wards off those aimed at him. The lance represents truth, and its pennon marks the fact that truth fears not falseness. There is no need to go further. Enough has been said to show the general nature of this fascinating if rather fruitless pastime of inventing symbolic significance for the various pieces of a knight's equipment. Undoubtedly whenever an aspirant to knighthood followed Lull's precepts so far as to expose himself to a sermon before he was dubbed, he heard some priest's private version of what his equipment signified.

As the ecclesiastical conception of chivalry reached its fullest elaboration in *Le libre del orde de cauayleria,* there is no need to discuss the vast number of fourteenth and fifteenth-century works which dealt with all or part of the ideas which composed it. The continued popularity of Lull's book and the insignificance of the changes made in it by translators and adaptors show that the ideas of religious chivalry underwent no important modification during these two centuries. As our next step is to examine how completely these ideas were accepted and put in practice by the nobles of France, it seems well to summarize them here. The basic concept of religious chivalry was the idea that the true knight as distinguished from the ordinary nobleman recognized certain obligations to God and the church and that these true knights formed the order of chivalry which was closely similar in nature to the clerical order. Its members upheld the church and the faith against all their foes. They protected the helpless and suppressed the violent. Furthermore they

practiced the Christian virtues and obeyed the commands of the church in every respect. In short the ecclesiastical writers and preachers simply took those precepts of feudal chivalry that did not conflict with the teachings of the church and added to them certain ideas which they considered all important. The latter as summarized above formed the concepts peculiar to religious chivalry.

An examination into the extent to which a set of ideals was accepted by a class of society is an extremely difficult task especially when that class was in general illiterate and left few statements of its ideas and motives. Historians have been inclined to search for a practice in accord with an idea and then calmly assume that the idea furnished the motive for the practice. The usual treatment of the crusades is an illustration of this tendency. The crusades have been pointed to as evidence of the influence of church ideas of chivalry on the mind of the feudal noble. Now it is perfectly true that if a knight accepted the precept of religious chivalry that it was his chief duty to protect the church from its foes, he might well feel obligated to go on a crusade, but the fact that he became a crusader did not prove that he would have considered himself no true knight had he not done so. Many purely secular motives could impel a noble to join a crusade. A younger son might hope to conquer a fief from the Moslems. A baron hard pressed by his neighbors might hope to gain the church's aid and protection. An unsuccessful rebel might flee the wrath of his lord. A restless and war-loving young noble who lived in a district where some feudal prince was effectively suppressing disorder might go to Spain or the Holy Land in search of adventure and opportunities to fight. In fact one could go on almost indefinitely listing plausible secular reasons why a knight might undertake a crusade and illustrate each one with the case of a noble who apparently had that motive.

To turn to religious motives the most obvious was the desire for salvation or more exactly for the spiritual indulgences promised crusaders. But there was nothing essentially chivalric about this motive —salvation was the fundamental object of all Christian life. The influence of the religious conception of chivalry can only be demonstrated by showing that nobles went crusading because they believed that their reputations as good knights demanded it. Now this idea is not entirely absent from the few documents which apparently expressed crusading motives, the poems written by departing crusaders. Conan of Béthune, who took part in the crusade of 1189, pointed out to the ladies who were left at home that if they were unfaithful to their absent lovers they would sin with cowards and worthless men for all good men would be on the crusade. An anonymous poem of about the same time stated that "God has called us to his aid and no worthy man should fail him." Count Thibaut of Champagne was more explicit.

All the worthless will stay here, those who love neither God, nor the good, nor honor, nor worth. . . . Now they will go, the valiant bachelors who love God and the glory of this world, those who wisely wish to go to God, and the useless, the cowards will remain. Blind indeed is he who does not make once in his life an expedition to succor God and who for so little loses the praise of the world.

The idea here is clear and definite. A noble who refused to crusade deserved to be considered a worthless knight.

Although the ideas of religious chivalry had some place in the minds of crusading nobles, no one who reads *Les chansons de croisade* collected by M. Bédier can feel that they had a very dominant influence. The search for salvation was clearly the chief and usually the sole religious motive. In this connection I cannot resist quoting a most illuminating passage from the troubadour Aimeric de Pégulhan.

Behold! without renouncing our rich garments, our station in life, courtesy, and all that pleases and charms we can obtain honor down here and joy in Paradise. To conquer glory by fine deeds and escape hell; what count or king could ask more? No more is there need to be tonsured or shaved and lead a hard life in the most strict order if we can revenge the shame which the Turks have done us. Is this not truly to conquer at once land and sky, reputation in the world and with God?

This may not represent the highest form of Christian enthusiasm, but I suspect that it gives a fair picture of the motives that moved most crusaders. In short while I have little doubt that the ideas of religious chivalry formed part of the mixture of reasons that led men to leave their homes to fight the infidel, it seems unlikely that chivalric conceptions were often the chief motives and their presence is practically impossible to demonstrate. Knights sought to save their souls by founding monasteries, going on pilgrimages, and fighting Moslems, but this furnishes little or no evidence as to how far they had accepted the chivalric ideas expressed by such writers as John of Salisbury and Ramon Lull.

If one turns to the rest of the extremely scanty supply of documents which can be said to represent the views of the noblemen of France, one may find here and there indications of the existence of these ideas. For instance the conception that a knight should be a policeman for the church seems to have had some currency. The biographer of William Marshal felt that his hero had acted in knightly fashion when he plundered a renegade monk of money that the latter intended to loan at usury. Joinville clearly approved of a knight who struck a Jew to the ground when he heard him uttering blasphemy. There was also apparently a feeling that a knight should not harm religious personages. Froissart viewed the burning of abbeys and raping of nuns as decidedly unworthy of good knights. The biographer of Marshal Boucicaut was much impressed by the Marshal's action in founding an order or fellowship of knights sworn to protect widows or other ladies in distress. Undoubtedly such items could be multiplied, but the meagerness of the material available would prevent the formation of any reasonably sound generalization.

At the same time it is certain that some precepts of religious chivalry never gained any acceptance among the feudal class. Obviously no professional warrior was going to develop an abhorrence of homicide. The church prohibited tournaments, but they continued to be considered by the nobles of France as the most proper occupation for a knight. In fact the Avignon popes who lived under the dominance of the chivalrous kings of the Valois line felt obliged to rescind their predecessors' decrees against this form of knightly sport. Finally it was useless for the church to preach against the taking of booty and ransoms. As William Marshal lay on his death bed, one of his knights pointed out to him that according to the teachings of the church no man could be saved who had not returned everything that he had taken from anyone. This did not worry the Marshal.

Henry, listen to me a while. The clerks are too hard on us. They shave us too closely. I have captured five hundred knights and have appropriated their arms, horses, and their entire equipment. If for this reason the kingdom of God is closed to me, I can do nothing about it, for I cannot return my booty. I can do no more for God than to give myself to him, repenting all my sins. Unless the clergy desire my damnation, they must ask no more. But their teaching is false—else no one could be saved.

Perhaps William was unusual in daring to question the validity of the church's teaching, but most of his contemporaries must have shared his disregard of its precepts on this question. Certainly I can find no evidence that any feudal noble felt that homicide committed in tourney or private war and the taking of booty and ransoms were anything but eminently proper in a knight.

As a matter of fact I am inclined to believe, though my evidence is quite tenuous, that the noble class abducted God from his position as founder and chief of religious chivalry and made him the patron of their own ideas on the subject. In the mind of Geoffrey of Villehardoin God was certainly on the side of the hardy knights who in defiance of the commands of pope, legate, and ordinary Christian decency captured the cities of Zara and Constantinople and had no use for the cowards who obeyed the church's order to go to Palestine. This was not, of course, very surprising. Soldiers have always been inclined to assume that God was on their side and have rarely failed to find priests to confirm their opinion. Particularly illuminating is the biographer of William Marshal's version of a speech delivered by Aimery de St. Maur, master of the Temple in England, as he stood by the bedside of the dying earl.

Marshal, attend. It pleases me that you give

yourself to God. He has granted you a great favor—that you will never be separated from Him. He has shown you this in your life, and He will do the same after your death. In the world you have had more honor than any other knight for prowess, wisdom, and loyalty. When God granted you His grace to this extent, you may be sure He wished to have you at the end. You depart from the age with honor. You have been a gentleman and you die one.

Add to this the words which the same author placed in the mouth of Stephen Langton, archbishop of Canterbury, as he preached the Marshal's funeral sermon:

Behold all that remains of the best knight who ever lived. . . . We have here our mirror, you and I. Let each man say his paternoster that God may receive this Christian into His Glory and place him among His faithful vassals, as he so well deserves.

Now William Marshal was no devotee of the ideas of religious chivalry. He had passed his life in industrious homicide in tourney and battle. For years he lived on ransoms won in tournaments. True, he had founded monasteries, but he had also plundered bishops. As these eloquent eulogies were being pronounced he lay under an excommunication launched by the bishop of Kilkenny. There can be no doubt that his biographer knew all this. To that anonymous writer who was so thoroughly imbued with the ideas of feudal chivalry it seemed impossible that God should not appreciate the virtues of a good knight. Prowess, wisdom, loyalty, generosity—what more could God ask?

On the whole it seems clear that the ideas of religious chivalry were current among the nobles of mediaeval France and may to some slight extent have modified their ethical conceptions. But it is certain that they never became so

dominant in the feudal mind that the ideal of knighthood propounded by the church replaced the one developed by the knights themselves. The men of the thirteenth, fourteenth, and fifteenth centuries who were admired by their contemporaries as models of knighthood were not perfect knights according to the ecclesiastical ideas. St. Louis who probably came as close to the church ideal as a living king could was admired as monarch and saint rather than as a knight. It was men like King Philip of Valois and his son John the Good, the Black Prince, and Bertrand du Guesclin who were considered the best knights of their day. In short the religious conception of chivalry made some impression on the mind of the feudal caste, but it never gained mastery over it. The virtues of feudal chivalry remained the qualities that were admired in a knight.

Obviously if I am correct in my belief that the ideas of religious chivalry made only a slight impression on the ethical conceptions of the nobility, they cannot have had much effect on its practices. Of course one could list an enormous number of nobles who went on crusades, but as I have attempted to show in a previous paragraph it is not necessary to believe that these ideas played any great part in persuading them to do so. Then most knights accepted without question the faith preached by the church and observed more or less carefully the established forms of the Christian cult. Many knights were pious, devout, and obedient Christians. But this could be said of the nobles of the eighth, ninth, and tenth centuries—it has little to do with chivalry. If the religious ideas of chivalry had ever been extensively practiced, one would expect to find a time when knights refrained from rapine and casual manslaughter, protected the church and its clergy, and respected the rights of helpless non-combatants in war. I can find no evidence that there ever was such a period. Many writers on the subject, both mediaeval and modern, have postulated a "golden age of chivalry" when the church's precepts were rigorously observed. Usually this glorious era has been placed in the twelfth century. Unfortunately twelfth-century writers like John of Salisbury and Stephen of Fougères were loud in their denunciations of the knights of their day, and other evidence thoroughly corroborates their statements. A case of some sort might be made for the claim that less regard was shown for human life and the persons and property of clergy and non-combatants in the fourteenth and fifteenth centuries than in the twelfth and thirteenth, but it would not be very convincing as a manifestation of chivalric decline. While it is possible to cite many more atrocities from the Hundred Years War than from the earlier period, one must remember that there is much more information available about the events of the later era. Then too the increase in the use of non-noble professional soldiers undoubtedly intensified the horrors of war. There seems no sound reason for believing that the knights of the later

Middle Ages observed the precepts of the church any less scrupulously than had their predecessors. In only one respect can one find evidence of definite variation in practice. From the middle of the twelfth century to the middle of the thirteenth the lives of noblemen appear to have been sacred except on the field of battle or the tourneying ground. Assassination and execution for political or criminal offenses was so rare as to be practically unknown. I can advance no explanation of this interesting phenomenon unless it be that the newly developed solidarity of the feudal caste had not yet succumbed to political necessities. At any rate there is no reason for connecting it with religious chivalry. Thus while it seems likely that individual knights were occasionally influenced in their practice by the ideals of chivalry propagated by churchmen, no grounds exist for believing that these ideas changed the behavior of the nobility as a whole. Religious chivalry as expressed by the writers of the Middle Ages has always appealed strongly to romantically inclined lovers of mankind. Virtue combined with might is perennially attractive. Nevertheless it seems probable that this fascinating conception was never much more than a pleasant dream.

In any effort to rank American medievalists according to their contribution to their chosen profession it would be difficult to find one more likely to head the list than CHARLES HOMER HASKINS (1870–1937). In *The Rise of Universities,* Haskins draws upon his vast learning in medieval institutional and intellectual history and provides a well-balanced and lucid account of the Middle Ages' most enduring contribution to the modern world.*

Charles Homer Haskins

The Universities of Northern Europe

In northern Europe the origin of universities must be sought at Paris, in the cathedral school of Notre-Dame. By the beginning of the twelfth century in France and the Low Countries learning was no longer confined to monasteries but had its most active centres in the schools attached to cathedrals, of which the most famous were those of Liège, Rheims, Laon, Paris, Orleans, and Chartres. The most notable of these schools of the liberal arts was probably Chartres, distinguished by a canonist like St. Ives and by famous teachers of classics and philosophy like Bernard and Thierry. As early as 991 a monk of Rheims, Richer, describes the hardships of his journey to Chartres in order to study the *Aphorisms* of Hippocrates of Cos; while from the twelfth century John of Salisbury, the leading northern humanist of the age, has left us an account of the masters. . . . Nowhere else today can we drop back more easily into a cathedral city of the twelfth century, the peaceful town still dominated by its church and sharing, now as then,

> the minister's vast repose.
> Silent and gray as forest-leaguered cliff
> Left inland by the ocean's slow retreat,
> . . . . patiently remote
> From the great tides of life it breasted once,
> Hearing the noise of men as in a dream.

By the time the cathedral stood complete, with its "dedicated shapes of saints and kings," it had ceased to be an intellectual centre of the first importance, overshadowed by Paris fifty-odd miles away, so that Chartres never became a university.

The advantages of Paris were partly geographical, partly political as the capital of the new French monarchy, but something must be set down to the influence of a great teacher in the person of Abelard. This brilliant young radical, with his persistent questioning and his scant respect for titled authority, drew students in large numbers wherever he taught, whether at Paris or in the wilderness. At Paris he was connected with the church of Mont-Sainte-Geneviève longer than with the cathedral school, but resort to Paris became a habit in his time, and in this way he had a significant influence on the rise of the university. In an institutional sense the university was a direct outgrowth of the school of Notre-Dame, whose chancellor alone had authority to license teaching in the diocese and thus kept his control over the granting of university degrees, which here as at Bologna were originally teachers' certificates. The early schools were within the cathedral precincts on the Ile de la Cité, that tangled quarter about Notre-Dame pictured by Victor Hugo which has long since been demolished. A little later we find masters and scholars living on the Little Bridge (Petit-Pont) which connected the island with the Left Bank of the Seine—this bridge gave its name to a whole school of philosophers, the Parvipontani—but by the thirteenth century they have overrun the Left Bank, thenceforth the Latin Quarter of Paris.

At what date Paris ceased to be a cathedral school and became a university, no one can say, though it was certainly before the end of the twelfth century. Universities, however, like to have precise dates to celebrate, and the University of Paris has chosen 1200, the year of its first royal charter. In that year, after certain students had been killed in a town and gown altercation, King Philip Augustus issued a formal privilege which punished his prévôt and recognized the exemption of the students and their servants from lay jurisdiction, thus creating that special position of students before the courts which has not yet wholly disappeared from the world's practice, though generally from its law. More specific was the first papal privilege, the bull *Parens scientiarum* of 1231, issued after a two years' cessation of lectures growing out of a riot in which a band of students, having found "wine that was good and sweet to drink" beat up the tavern keeper and his friends till they in turn suffered from the prévôt and his men, a dissension in which the thirteenth century clearly saw the hand of the devil. Confirming the existing exemptions, the Pope goes on to regulate the discretion of the chancellor in conferring the license, at the same time that he recognizes the right of the masters and students "to make constitutions and ordinances regulating the manner and time of lectures and disputations, the costume to be worn," attendance at masters' funerals, the lectures of bachelors, necessarily more limited than those of fully fledged masters, the price of lodgings, and the coercion of members. Students must not carry arms, and only those who frequent the schools regularly are to enjoy the exemptions of students, the interpretation in practice being attendance at not less than two lectures a week.

While the word university does not appear in these documents, it is taken for granted. A university in the sense of an organized body of masters existed already in the twelfth century; by 1231 it had developed into a corporation, for Paris, in contrast to Bologna, was a university of masters. There were now four faculties, each under a dean: arts, canon law (civil law was forbidden at Paris after 1219), medicine, and theology. The masters of arts, much more numerous than the others, were grouped into four "nations": the French, including the Latin peoples; the Normans; the Picard, including also the Low Countries; and the English, comprising England, Germany, and the North and East of Europe. These four nations chose the head of the university, the rector, as he is still generally styled on the Continent, whose term, however, was short, being later only three months. If we may judge from such minutes as have survived, much of the time of the nations was devoted to consuming the fees collected from new members and new officers, or, as it was called, drinking up the surplus—at the Two Swords near the Petit-Pont, at the sign of Our Lady in the Rue S.-Jacques, at the Swan, the Falcon, the Arms of France, and scores of similar places. A learned monograph on the taverns of mediaeval Paris has been written from the records of the English nation alone. The artificial constitution of the nations seems to have encouraged rather than diminished the feuds and rivalries between the various regions represented at Paris, of which Jacques de Vitry has left a classic description:

They wrangled and disputed not merely about the various sects or about some discussions; but the differences between the countries also caused dissensions, hatreds, and virulent animosities among them, and they impudently uttered all kinds of affronts and insults against one another. They affirmed that the English were drunkards and had tails; the sons of France proud, effeminate, and carefully adorned like women. They said that the Germans were furious and obscene at their feasts; the Normans, vain and boastful; the Poitevins, traitors and always adventurers. The Bur-

gundians they considered vulgar and stupid. The Bretons were reputed to be fickle and changeable, and were often reproached for the death of Arthur. The Lombards were called avaricious, vicious, and cowardly; the Romans, seditious, turbulent, and slanderous; the Sicilians, tyrannical and cruel; the inhabitants of Brabant, men of blood, incendiaries, brigands, and ravishers; the Flemish, fickle, prodigal, gluttonous, yielding as butter, and slothful. After such insults, from words they often came to blows.

Another university institution which goes back to twelfth-century Paris is the college. Originally merely an endowed hospice or hall of residence, the college early became an established unit of academic life at many universities. "The object of the earliest college-founders was simply to secure board and lodging for poor scholars who could not pay for it themselves"; but in course of time the colleges became normal centres of life and teaching, absorbing into themselves much of the activity of the university. The colleges had buildings and endowments, if the university had not. There was a college at Paris as early as 1180; there were sixty-eight by 1500, and the system survived until the Revolution, to leave behind it only fragments of buildings or local names like the Sorbonne of today, sole memento of that Collège de la Sorbonne founded for theologians by a confessor of St. Louis in the thirteenth century. Many other continental universities had their colleges, one of which, the ancient College of Spain at Bologna, still survives for the delectation of the few Spanish youths who reach its quiet courtyard. But of course the ultimate home of the college was Oxford and Cambridge, where it came to be the most characteristic feature of university life, arrogating to itself practically all teaching as well as direction of social life, until the university became merely an examining and degree-conferring body. Here the older colleges like Balliol, Merton, and Peterhouse date from the thirteenth century.

Paris was pre-eminent in the Middle Ages as a school of theology, and, as theology was the supreme subject of mediaeval study, "Madame la haute science" it was called, this means that it was pre-eminent as a university. "The Italians have the Papacy, the Germans have the Empire, and the French have Learning," ran the old saying; and the chosen abode of learning was Paris. Quite naturally Paris became the source and the model for northern universities. Oxford branched off from this parent stem late in the twelfth century, likewise with no definite date of foundation; Cambridge began somewhat later. The German universities, none of them older than the fourteenth century, were confessed imitations of Paris. Thus the Elector Palatine, Ruprecht, in founding the University of Heidelberg in 1386—for these later universities were founded at specific dates—provides that it "shall be ruled, disposed, and regulated according to the modes and matters accustomed to be observed in the University of Paris, and that as a handmaid of Paris—a worthy one let us hope—it shall imitate the steps of Paris in every way possible, so that there shall be four faculties," four nations and a rector, exemptions for students and their servants, and even caps and gowns for the several faculties "as has been observed at Paris."

By the end of the Middle Ages at least eighty universities had been founded in different parts of Europe. Some of these were short-lived, many were of only local importance, others like Salerno flourished only to die, but some like Paris and Montpellier, Bologna and Padua, Oxford

and Cambridge, Vienna and Prague and Leipzig, Coimbra and Salamanca, Cracow and Louvain, have an unbroken history of many centuries of distinction. And the great European universities of more recent foundation, like Berlin, Strasbourg, Edinburgh, Manchester, and London, follow in their organization the ancient models. In America the earliest institutions of higher learning reproduced the type of the contemporary English college at a time when the university in England was eclipsed by its constituent colleges; but in the creation of universities in the later nineteenth century, America turned to the universities of the Continent and thus entered once more into the ancient inheritance. Even in the colonial period a sense of the general university tradition survived, for the charter of Rhode Island College in 1764 grants "the same privileges, dignities, and immunities enjoyed by the American colleges, and European universities."

What then is our inheritance from the oldest of universities? In the first place it is not buildings or a type of architecture, for the early universities had no buildings of their own, but on occasion used private halls and neighboring churches. After all, as late as 1775 the First Baptist Church in Providence was built "for the publick worship of Almighty God, and also for holding Commencement in"! Indeed one who seeks to reconstruct the life of ancient universities will find little aid in their existing remains. Salerno retains no monuments of its university, though its rare old cathedral, where Hildebrand lies buried, must have seen the passing of many generations of would-be physicians. In the halls and coats of arms of "many-domed Padua proud" we behold the Renaissance, not the Middle Ages. Even Bologna, *Bononia docta*, with its leaning towers and cool arcades, has no remains of university architecture earlier than the fourteenth century, from which date the oldest monuments of its professors of law gathered now into the municipal museum. Montpellier and Orleans preserve nothing from this period. Paris, too often careless of its storied past, can show today only the ancient church of Saint-Julien-le-Pauvre, where university meetings were often held, unless we count, as we should, the great cathedral in the Cité whence the university originally sprang. The oldest Cambridge college, Peterhouse, has only a fragment of its earliest buildings; the finest Cambridge monument, King's College chapel, is of the late fifteenth century. More than all others Oxford gives the deepest impression of continuity with an ancient past, Matthew Arnold's Oxford, "so venerable, so lovely . . . steeped in sentiment as she lies, spreading her gardens to the moonlight, and whispering from her towers the last enchantments of the Middle Age"; yet so far as the actual college buildings are concerned they have much more of sentiment than of the Middle Ages. Only at Merton, which fixed the college type at Oxford, do any of the present structures carry us back of 1300, and nowhere is there much of the fourteenth century. Those venerable glories of Oxford, the Bodleian library, the tower of Magdalen, and the hall of Christ Church, belong to a much later age, the period of the Tudors, and thus by ordinary reckoning to modern times. When we say how very mediaeval, we often mean how very Tudor!

Neither does the continuity lie in academic form and ceremony, in spite of occasional survivals, like the conferring of degrees by the ring or the kiss of peace, or the timing of examinations by the hour glass as I have seen it at Portuguese Coimbra. Academic costume has in it some element of tradition where it is a daily dress as at Oxford, Cambridge, and Coimbra, but in America the tradition was broken by our ancestors, and the formal cap and gown current in the United States today are a product of modern Albany rather than of mediaeval Paris and Bologna. Even in their ancient homes the costumes have changed. "It is probable," says Rashdall, "that no gown now worn in Oxford has much resemblance to its mediaeval ancestor." A student of mediaeval Padua would not recognize the variegated procession which wound through its streets last summer; Robert de Sorbon would rub his eyes at the non-mediaeval styles of the gorgeous gowns which were massed on the stage of the great hall of the Sorbonne when President Wilson received his honorary degree in 1918.

It is, then, in institutions that the university tradition is most direct. First, the very name university, as an association of masters and scholars leading the common life of learning. Characteristic of the Middle Ages as such a corporation is, the individualistic modern world has found nothing to take its place. Next, the notion of a curriculum of study, definitely laid down as regards time and subjects, tested by an examination and leading to a degree, as well as many of the degrees themselves—bachelor, as a stage toward the mastership, master, doctor, in arts, law, medicine, and theology. Then the faculties, four or more, with their deans, and the higher officers such as chancellors and rectors, not to mention the college, wherever the residential college still survives. The essentials of university organization are clear and unmistakable, and they have been handed down in unbroken continuity. They have lasted more than seven hundred years—what form of government has lasted so long? Very likely all this is not final—nothing is in this world of flux—but it is singularly tough and persistent, suited to use and also to abuse, like Bryce's university with a faculty "consisting of Mrs. Johnson and myself," or the "eleven leading universities" of a certain state of the Middle West! Universities are at times criticised for their aloofness or their devotion to vocationalism, for being too easy or too severe, and drastic efforts have been made to reform them by abolishing entrance requirements or eliminating all that does not lead directly to bread and butter; but no substitute has been found for the university in its main business, the training of scholars and the maintenance of the tradition of learning and investigation. The glory of the mediaeval university, says Rashdall, was "the consecration of Learning," and the glory and the vision have not yet perished from the earth. "The mediaeval university," it has been said, "was the school of the modern spirit."

The popular image of the Church as an inflexible institution bound by age-old traditions is attacked by JOHN GILCHRIST in *The Church and Economic Activity in the Middle Ages*. Gilchrist points out that in economic life at least, the Church was adaptable and a policymaker of great importance. His primary aim, however, is to illuminate the relation between the Church's teaching on economic matters and its activities in that sphere.*

John Gilchrist

The Church and the Medieval Economy

Church Property and Organization

The most noteworthy feature of the reformed canon law of the eleventh century onwards, as far as economic matters are concerned, is the stress put upon the preservation of ecclesiastical property. All in all, according to David Herlihy, there was *c.* 1050–1120 an 80 per cent decrease in land transfers, a process especially marked in Italy, Spain and France.

The concept of the inalienability of ecclesiastical lands was connected with a moral aim to eliminate priest-marriage and to abolish simony. Special provision had to be made for a celibate clergy, and lands·that had been lost to lay relatives

and to secular powers had to be recovered and retained. Consequently the Church began to hold on to its land, a policy emulated by laymen, who bought up scattered pieces and consolidated them into large estates. In an interesting study Herlihy attributes the influence of the Church in raising the status of married women as one reason why eleventh-century women became prominent as landholders. This policy of buying also stimulated the money-market. There was a need for cash. High interest rates were offered. Money and treasure that had been hoarded came out in response. Herlihy gives an excellent example of this stimulation of the money-market in the case of Italy, where 40 per cent of

*From John Gilchrist, *The Church and Economic Activity in the Middle Ages* (London: Macmillan and Company, Ltd., 1969), pp. 99–121. Reprinted by permission of Macmillan and Company, Ltd., and St. Martin's Press, Inc. Footnotes omitted.

contracts for land purchase involved payment of substitute money—gold ornaments, jewellery, furs, swords and armour. The peak of the movement was about 1038–70, but it lasted for another fifty years.

An interesting aspect of the Church's land-buying policy is that it created surplus labour. This was especially noticeable on Cistercian estates during the twelfth century. At the beginning the impetus was healthy. Redundant labour had to re-locate itself, thus supplying a work force for the new towns and contributing to the demand for goods, which were decisive factors in the economic expansion of the time.

The demand for goods came both from a rising standard of living, and from the population increases from *c.* 1000 onwards. This raises the question of how far the Church's teaching on marriage favoured the increase. Josiah C. Russell's view is that "ecclesiastical policies favoured increasing population." Ecclesiastical authors wrote against abortion and infanticide. They also stressed the positive injunction "increase and multiply." From these developments came also the disappearance of slavery in Catholic Europe.

More especially, the impact of legislation of the Church in relation to its own economy may be judged by examining its success in reclaiming tithes. After an unsuccessful period of trying to recover the whole of the tithes that had been lost to the Church, the popes adopted a more realistic approach. Lateran IV 32 recognized that only a portion of the tithe could be recovered—the parish priest's. In parts of Europe the Church successfully implemented this decree. In northern Italy it was almost universally successful. It ensured a minimum revenue for the parish clergy, some independence from lay influence, and also met with the approval of laymen who "saw not only justice but also advantage in a reform that still left three-quarters in their own hands."

In the later Middle Ages, however, the collection of tithes became difficult. Already many predial tithes had been commuted for money. Lay persons and religious had got control of others, and the friars often encouraged the faithful not to pay their tithe to their ill-educated priest, but to give it to charity or to the friars themselves. The wills of London citizens testify to this evasion of tithe-payment. Many wills (some seven out of ten) open with a bequest to the testator's parish church "in payment of tithes and offerings withheld." The sums restored range from a few pence by workers to the £ 10 or £ 20 of the wealthy capitalist.

A similar success attended the papacy's attempt to persuade the religious Orders to appoint perpetual vicars to churches held by them. . . . The records of the Abbey of Saint-Vincent-du-Mans provide a specific example of restoration of sequestrated parish-church revenues to the parish priest. The process began with the cure of Sables in 1220 and then extended to churches of Beton, Doucelles, Saint-Ouen de Ballon, Saint-Croneille and Saint-Patrice-du-Désert et-Marolettes.

This type of compromise was a realistic appraisal of the possible. Three centuries later Lateran V, instead of attempting a similar compromise on matters affecting Church and State, pursued the extremist line of clerical independence. This happened on the eve of the Reformation. Yet churchmen were not entirely to blame. If the canonist had failed to evolve new financial teachings to cater for the needs of the secular states, the latter had not suffered any serious loss of income. Recent work by Peter Partner and William L. Lunt, among others, has shown that from the fourteenth century the princes forced the papacy to grant them an ever-increasing share of church revenues. The odium of exacting these sums fell on the Church and its agents, which became a further weapon with which the secular powers could undermine papal authority. In the period of the Reformation, denunciation by the Protestant reformers of papal exactions was common, but propaganda glossed over the part that the princes had played in maintaining and fostering those same ideas.

These facts do not constitute a defence of papal policy and action in the later Middle Ages. The Renaissance popes, like other Renaissance princes, proved their efficiency by exploiting all possible sources of revenue, by transforming, in the fifteenth century, the once free communes of the papal states into units of authoritarian papal rule. To their aid they brought the spiritual weapon of excommunication, even to force debtors to repay their loans, as Pius II in his *Commentaries* shows on a few occasions. Like any Renaissance prince the pope monopolized the sale of such basic commodities as salt. He was also quick to seize the advantages of the discovery of alum on papal lands at Tolfa in 1460. Having entered a partnership with the Medici for its production, the papacy then tried to remove the competition of imported Turkish alum. To pay its hired soldiers it sometimes granted assignments of the tallage of its towns with right to pillage if the town defaulted. For that day and age these procedures ranked as acceptable business methods, for a later age they have become sources of accusation and sometimes scorn.

In general the critics of the medieval Church fasten too easily upon the later events and failures. They overlook, for example, the way in which the Church nurtured the growth of civil liberties "in a large number of towns from Worms to Tournai" in the tenth century, and that these became the basis for the municipal liberties of the twelfth century. Out of the constant conflict between Church and State, even at the economic level, was born that sense of constitutionalism that came to be part of the medieval heritage. Also, the papacy introduced new methods of taxation, especially as part of its programme to help finance the crusades, which showed the national states how to tax income and goods as well as land. Nor should it be forgotten that, in the thirteenth century, in land-holding the Church contributed to the development of the life-lease in contrast to perpetual leases. This avoided the constant danger of loss of lands and gave some hope of future reversion.

Passing from the papacy to the monasteries, the most important, and still much debated, question concerns the influence of the monastic economy within the various European states, especially of the Cistercian Order. The latter has been heavily criticized in recent years, but this criticism is directed against their business dealings in the later period. These, thanks to the work of scholars such as R. A. Donkin, are today commonly known and documented. The later abuses tend to overshadow the benefits conferred during the early years, which should not be forgotten. For example, in England, many of the seventy-seven abbeys were founded in underdeveloped or neglected, but potentially fertile, regions such as northeast Yorkshire, which was "waste" and bog, and which had been depopulated after the Norman Conquest. The Order preferred such areas because there were no feudal dues, tithes to pay or other financial burdens. Also the laity were more likely to grant "waste" lands than existing profitable estates. Using the system of the monastic grange, largely run by lay brothers, the monks furthered the development of these areas. Consequently they were in the forefront of, and some would say they began, large-scale wool production in England as others did elsewhere. By sponsoring the fulling mill they contributed to the English cloth trade, although they themselves did not reap the benefits of these things. Later, things were different. Depopulation of estates, conversion of arable to pasture, tithe disputes with the secular clergy and the Benedictine monasteries led to bitter wrangling that needed conciliar legislation to settle. . . . The economic prosperity of the Order led them to such abuse of their privileges as the marketing of non-monastic wool. In 1262 the Crown issued royal mandates warning the Cistercian abbots in Lincolnshire about putting other men's wool with their own to avoid payment of customs. Similar injunctions of 1275 accused the Cistercians of Louth Park, Kirkstead and Revesby of having bought up wool and other produce over a period of fifteen years in order to sell to foreign merchants. As a result Lincoln had lost 100 marks of customs dues. The monks obviously disregarded the warning, for in 1302 the Commons of Lincolnshire complained that "men of religion drove a wool trade, not only in produce of their own sheep, but by sending men out to buy cheap in order to sell dear." The action of the Cistercians is equally explicable on economic grounds, for, as C. V. Graves suggests, the occurrence of the scab among sheep from 1277 onwards caught the monks with no means of fulfilling long-term contracts for supply of wool. They had to buy from outside sources. Nor did they make much profit. They had to buy short on borrowed money, and so began the circle of debt and yet more debt.

Monastic, especially Cistercian, involvement in large-scale business activities was a sorry affair. The methods they used were often reprehensible, even to laymen. In particular one may remark on the large-scale recruitment of the *conversi* and hired labour. Proportionately these *conversi* and hired labourers were the mainstay of the Order. The Cistercian abbey of Beaulieu in the thirteenth century had some 58 professed monks and about 150 lay brothers as well as the hired labour. In the fourteenth century, Canterbury cathedral priory had 25 obedientiaries, many with their own household, and by 1400 there were twice as many servants as monks at the abbey. Maintenance of such large numbers, as well as the monks' expensive tastes, such as imported best Flemish cloth for their dress, created serious financial problems for the abbey. Moreover, many of the monastic commercial practices antagonized the rest of the countryside as well as the merchants. They smacked of those monopolies forbidden by the canonists. Then there is some evidence, in England at least, that the abbeys acquired cheaply lands that had been given as security to the Jewish money-lenders, hence the presence of the Jews could be an advantage as much as a disadvantage. Again the Cistercians used their privilege of exemption from paying customs duties and tolls to transport the goods of other merchants. Such exploitation of their economic strength left the religious Orders without defenders during the later Middle Ages.

A last question about the monks is the degree to which they influenced farming methods. The cumulative impression left by the study of a number of individual monasteries is that we may have underestimated the monastic example. Canterbury cathedral priory had several manuals of husbandry for its use in the late thirteenth century, including four manuscripts of the celebrated treatise by Walter of Henley. The registers contain frequent references to it. The financial administrators, the *seniores ad scaccarium,* especially under the priorate of Henry of Eastry (1285–1331), project an image of careful management of resources; they give attention to such problems as the sale of corn, care of sheep and cattle, marling of land, and the purchase of seed grain from other parts rather than using less productive strains of their own growth.

Negatively, the business acumen of the monks may have helped to undermine objections the laity may have had to adopting a loose interpretation of the Church's teaching. In other words, clerical and monastic example proved more powerful than doctrine.

Profit and Usury

One area in which the ecclesiastical economy did not have much *direct* effect was in the establishment of its own monetary institutions. Despite the emergence of the Order of Templars as an international banking organization, the Church authorities relied mainly on lay banks. The papacy, especially, preferred Italian merchants and bankers. Until the crash of 1345–6 they used the Peruzzi, Bardi, Bonaccorsi and Acciaiuoli; next the Alberti until 1376, then the Guinigi of Lucca, and between 1401 and 1494 the Medici. Merchant-bankers were frequently charged with the task of collecting the crusade tenths as well as other dues from princes, laity and clergy. They also acted as "supply merchants, money-changers, postal agents, agents of information" and even as unofficial legates. In these matters the papacy showed itself extremely businesslike. For example,

whenever it thought a clerical escort would provide a cheaper method than bank transfer for moving money, e.g. from France to Lombardy, an escort was used.

Lesser institutions and individuals also preferred lay money-lenders and bankers. No special distinction was made between Jew and Christian, foreign and local, until the later Middle Ages. In 1213 Canterbury cathedral priory negotiated a number of loans for long terms and at high rates of interest. The creditors included Jews of the towns as well as Italian merchants of various cities of origin, such as Rome, Siena, Bologna, Florence and Pistoia. The rate of interest varied from 15 to 20 per cent. Eventually, by the time of the priorate of Henry of Eastry (1285–1331), Jew had given way to Christian and foreign to local capital. Cluny, under Peter the Venerable *c.* 1125, resorted to Jewish usurers at Mâcon, and gave, contrary to canon law, church ornaments as a pawn. In 1149 the abbey owed 2000 marks of silver and preferred to borrow from the Christian merchants. The abbey of Bury St Edmunds in the time of Abbot Hugh used Jewish usuries at a rate of interest by which "a debt of forty marks increased to one hundred pounds." The Jew Aaron of Lincoln had among his debtors the Abbot of Westminster, the Prior of the Hospitallers, the bishops of Lincoln and Bangor, and the archdeacons of Colchester and Carlisle. The debts ranged from the Archbishop of Canterbury's 100 marks to John, priest of St Margaret's, debt of 4s.

Upon the lay banking-companies the Church exerted a great deal of power and influence. But this was surpassed by the effect of its usury doctrine of which Raymond De Roover writes:

Since the bankers, in this regard, tried as much as possible to comply with religious precepts, they had to operate without incurring the censure of the theologians. As a result, banking in the Middle Ages and even much later—on the continent until far into the eighteenth century—was quite different from what it is today. It would be erroneous to believe that the usury doctrine was simply disregarded and had scarcely any effect on banking practices.

On usury in the narrow sense of the word the effectiveness of canonist doctrine depended on the willing support of the bishops and clergy and the secular authorities. . . . Lateran IV 6 recognized the importance of provincial and diocesan synods by having bishops in their assembly read the decrees of the council. From the examples of France and England, where the basic research has already been done, it is clear that in the thirteenth century the decrees of local synods largely followed those of the general council; thus the canons on usury were repeated in France at the local councils of Avignon 1209 and 1282, Saint-Quentin 1231, Château-Gontier 1232, Albi 1254, Sens 1269, Pont-Audemer 1279, Tours 1282, Bourges 1286. The council of Pont-Audemer ordered the usury canon . . . to be read in parish churches every Sunday. The crusade provisions of Lateran IV [71], . . . Lyons [5], and . . . Lyons II [1c], were ordered to be read in the coastal towns on Sundays and feast days.

The "success" and "failure" of this policy can be seen in several regions. Toulouse provides a prime example. Here there was a long history of concealed usury, from the second half of the tenth century onwards. The commonest form was the *mortgage,* which lasted from the tenth to the twelfth century. About the middle of the twelfth century, the system changed, In 1163 came the first instance of an open loan in which the interest is clearly a charge on the debt. From 1184 there are plenty of examples of such loans, and the next three or four decades have

been called the golden age of usurers at Toulouse. But this "golden age" began to change with the advent of Fulk as Bishop of Toulouse (1205–31). He found the episcopal lands deep in debt or pledged to creditors. Quite rightly, he attributed some of these happenings to the lax usury laws. As a remedy he created a special tribunal of two judges "to hear complaints and charges of usury," and this tribunal forced the usurers to make restitution. Under pressure of this sort, interest agreements tended to disappear, certainly from the notarial records. Usurers, when they applied to the courts to have repayment of a debt enforced, claimed compensation for damages caused by delay in repayment, with the clause added *preter usuram.* In practice, usury continued at Toulouse. The merchants tried to avoid open usury and instead resorted to fictitious deals, e.g. loans of wheat (in fact, only money changed hands) made at a lower than market price and repaid later (again in money) at the current price. Similar transactions are recorded at Brussels.

In the matter of usury, appeasement of conscience became easier as one ascended the social scale, for consumption loans were less common. Better security was available, and most loans could be concealed in one form or another, or even genuinely made by reason of the risk element. For despite the great learning and polished exposition of the canonists and theologians, the fact remains that the Church from the twelfth to the sixteenth century, from the lowest clergy to the papacy, existed by some form of credit financing. One can only cite examples. Hubert, Bishop of Limerick (1223–50), borrowed 166 marks from the Roman firm of Manetti. He repaid 60 marks on 20 February 1229, but having failed to pay the balance he was excommunicated and forced to make "a new agreement before the papal judge." In 1237 he repaid not the 106 marks owing, but 160 marks, that is, 54 marks interest over eight years. The Irish clergy, in order to pay the huge aids and subsidies levied on them, resorted to the Italian bankers, and they usually had papal consent to contract the loans. Consequently the sees of Armagh and Cashel were in debt during the second half of the thirteenth century. In 1324 in London a group of city merchants appear as creditors of abbeys and priories throughout England. The institutions repaid their debts by granting annuities, thus the Prior of the Order of St John gave annuities to the families of Oxford and Rothing. John of Oxford, as well as being a successful wine merchant, was creditor of twenty-one religious houses. For London in the period 1324–44 recognizances of some twenty houses had a total value of £ 8000. In France the Avignonese papacy had frequent dealings with its bankers, not merely for exchange purposes, but also as a creditor and sometimes as a debtor. In theory the papal Curia did not pay interest on its loans. The bulls speak of loans made *gratuite et amicabiliter.* The reality was different. Vague terms such as *cum cambio* were used to disguise the fact of interest. There was probably no real difficulty here, for the majority of canonists held that it was not unlawful to pay interest in case of necessity. At Cologne in 1388 the Lombards lent the archbishop money with the tax revenues as a pledge. In other words, they became tax-farmers. One Ambrosius paid a weekly sum of 250 marks to farm the *Mahlpfennig.*

The evidence of Lyons I [1] suggests that usury *had* become a problem that seriously affected the clergy. The latter, instead of paying off debts and running their parishes economically, had plunged into debt (especially over lavish building programmes) and taken out mortgages on property. Several decrees prohibit the pawning of sacred objects, which in itself exemplifies the actions of the clergy. To prevent this, Lyons I [1] revived or rather enforced more strictly the acient rule that an inventory should be made, on assuming office, of property, furnishings and debts, and immediate provision made to pay off the debts, especially those that were "usurious or burdensome." No debts were to be contracted in future, except with consent. In any case no debts were to be contracted on the open market—presumably, that is, with manifest usurers —to avoid excessive rates and public scandal. Annual accounts were to be rendered.

Despite the deep involvement of churchmen in borrowing and lending, the laws as far as laity were concerned were not allowed to remain dead letters. Research into restitutions made by usurers gives some interesting conclusions. Firstly, the canonists distinguished between restoring usurious gains that were *certa,* that is, to the borrowers or their families who were known, and *incerta,* which would go to the Church for charitable purposes. With public or manifest usurers there was no problem. They could be, and were, taken before church courts and forced to make restitution unless, as often happened, the secular authority protected then, e.g. by licence. The comparative ease with which the ecclesiastical courts could deal with this class of usurer tended to make them overlook the occult usurer and the large-scale investor, who in any case by 1350 and onwards were well covered by the doctrine of exceptions and and the concept of *lucrum cessans* and *damnum emergens.*

In the end the various conciliar and local synodal decrees caught mostly only the pawnbrokers. In the case of the merchant *élite,* who during their life at least seemed to escape the penalties of usury laws, the one saving condition is that they too lived in an age of religious belief, in which to save one's soul was the ultimate reality. Men could acquire riches and great wealth, but they could not escape the mute accusation of having broken some law. These men the Church could reach through fear of the final judgement. An outstanding example of this is the Merchant of Prato, for whom "with old age came the last and worst anxiety: overwhelming fear of what would happen to him in a future life. Pilgrimages and periods of fasting, gifts of pictures to churches and of lands to convents, and, finally, the bestowal of all his great fortune to charitable works—none of these sufficed to dispel the haunting sense of guilt that darkened his last years—a gnawing anguish, a perpetual *maninconia* [*sic*]." In merchant-banker wills of the twelfth to the early fourteenth centuries there are many and significant examples of restitution, mostly of the *certa* type. An excellent example of restitution is the following document dated Lucca, 13 March 1220:

Ugolino and Arduino, brothers, [sons] of the late Ildebrandino, feeling weighed down by usuries which Genovese, [recently] deceased, had extracted from them, therefore appealed to the Supreme Pontiff, [asking] that Filippo, priest [and] rector of the Church of S. Pietro Somaldi, must not bury him before they are satisfied in regard to the usuries which they had asked him to return. This was done in Lucca, in the court of S. Pietro Somaldi, in the portico, in the presence of Gaiascone, [son] of the late Orlando Guasone, and of Guido, [son] of the late Orlandino, 1220, the third [day] before the Ides of March. [I], Benedetto, judge and notary of the lord emperor, took part in this entire [transaction] and I wrote this as a record.

The merchants who made such loans were mainly Italian, their debtors, who mostly benefited from the last pangs of conscience, were usually from across the Alps. They included a variety of individuals, bishop as well as knight, and corporations, monastic or cathedral chapter and local guilds. In one of his bulls John XXII "refers to two brothers of Asti, who are obligated to restore 60,000 gold florins for usuries abroad." Lyons II 27 admitted the right of the ordinary to fix the amount owing in restitution, but the popes often intervened in the case of prominent usurers, especially their own creditors. The *incerta* could be granted where the bishop or pope wished. So this provided a useful source of additional income. Not surprisingly, the proportion of *certa* to *incerta* tended to decrease in this period.

The paradox of the Church as a viable, corporate society, subject to the reality of economic problems as any other secular body, and as a divinely instituted society, is seen in the history of Lyons II 26 and 27. These two decrees originally formed a single text, which provides a curious document on usury and makes it worthy of comment at length.

This legislation on usury is generally accepted as "of far-reaching importance . . . in the history of the later Middle Ages." By showing the changes that the text underwent between the time of promulgation by the council and publication by the pope, it is possible to learn a great deal about the then contemporary attitude towards usury. The two main changes are very significant. First, the draft version found in MS Washington 183 (Catholic University of America) prohibited usurers *in general* from hiring or leasing suitable business premises. The published text, however, added a qualifying clause "alienigenas et alios non oriundos de terris ipsorum," which means, in effect, that only foreign usurers were expressly denied right of carrying on their business. The second point is that the published version increased the penalties for public usurers by adding the clause "Testamenta quoque manifestorum usurariorum aliter facta non valeant, sed sint irrita ipso iure" (Wills of notorious usurers that make no reference to this point are *ipso iure* invalid).

These changes mean that the *foreign* and public usurer was regarded as the main culprit. Guillelmus Durandus (*c.* 1230–96) in fact "explained that the canon was not meant to extend to occult usurers or to native practitioners, even though public, but to the foreign manifest usurers like the Sienese and Florentines in England, and those who were called *prestatores, cahorsins* and *renovatores* in Italy, France and Provence respectively." Confirmation comes from the report of Franciscus de Albano on the Lyons council. The report informs us that the council had been "asked specifically to curb the activities of the travelling merchants from Florence, Siena, Pistoia, Lucca and Asti," who went about the various regions exacting quite exorbitant rates of interest. Of course, it has to be kept in mind that foreign usurers and merchants roused hostile feelings because they stood for competition and sometimes financial loss. In 1284 the citizens of Lincoln complained that foreign merchants displayed their wares in near-by places and deprived the city of revenues.

The *glossa ordinaria* (on Lyons II 26) added that native usurers were open to other forms of punishment, but in any case they never did as much harm as foreigners. But mainly, I think, the legislation was aimed at the Lombards, the pawnbrokers. In practice a Venetian prohibition of 1281 against foreigners carrying on money-lending activities in the state points to this conclusion, for, as we shall see, moderate interest on loans by local citizens was favourably regarded.

As for the punishment of usurers, the papacy's action in adding the clause invalidating the wills of those who refused to provide for restitution later caused a great deal of controversy. Admittedly the clergy could refuse to attend or witness the drawing-up of a will, but by what authority could the Church invalidate it? Gregory X had a precedent—a canon of the council of Paris in 1212–and, as mentioned above, a powerful reason, but the clause created further tension between lay and clerical authorities. And it was also put to profit, for, despite the provision of Vienne [29] denouncing states that licensed (for a price) usurers, the latter could always purchase papal exemption from the sentence of excommunication.

The question of restitution by Jews was a more difficult one. Initially the Deuteronomy provision had protected their position as the leading pawnbrokers in a Christian society. But in the thirteenth century some theologians had questioned Jewish exemption from the general scriptural prohibition of usury. This, no doubt, is why the records of Jewish usurers at Perpignan include appeals by Christians to the courts for restitution. Against this, the lay power's interest lay in protecting the Jew against such suits.

In some countries Jewish usurers disappeared altogether after the thirteenth century, but in traditional areas, such as Italy, they preserved their position. Several communes made agreements with the Jews to open loan banks *(banchi di pegno)*. They first appeared in the duchy of Mantua in 1380 and lasted until 1808. In the sixteenth century the duchy had forty such "banks." At Orvieto the Jews had privileges dating from a special statute in 1312, which made them true citizens, gave them rights of seizure of their debtors' goods, if necessary, and imprisonment until the debt was paid. For these privileges the Jews paid heavily. An individual Jew could pay an annual tax of between 10 and 100 livres at a time when the biggest guild paid only 50 livres. After the Black Death the Jews felt secure enough to sue for recovery of debts from heirs of their now defunct debtors. The commune granted one-quarter of such debts to be collected, and prevented subsequent abuses by Orvietans, but rather than get involved, the Jewish money-lenders were often willing to settle out of court. Vienne [29] is said to have implicitly condemned the Jewish claim that the double standard of Deuteronomy permitted them to exact usury from Christians, together with the secular authorities who enforced their claims against debtors. Against this is the papal dispensation that sanctioned Jewish money-lending in Christian communities, e.g. Nicholas V in 1452, granted Lucca the right to have "unum, vel plures Iudeum seu Iudeos feneratores" to provide consumer credit.

From around 1350 the number of explicit restitutions of usuries in the wills of prominent merchants, whether of *certa* or *incerta,* declined absolutely. This indicates a change in the authority of the Church and in the attitude of the merchant classes. As long as the Church and municipal authorities had been in accord, the latter supported the jurisdiction of the church courts. In Florence, before the outbreak in 1345–6 of hostilities between the papacy and the Republic, the secular tribunals accepted ecclesiastical verdicts without reservation. Then came the financial crash. In 1343 the great Florentine banks were on the verge of bankruptcy. The Avignonese papacy, instead of help-

ing them, abandoned them. The papal inquisitor Piero dell'Aguila also had arrested Salvestro Baroncelli, a partner in the Acciaiuoli Company, who owed money to the Church, and he fined heavily those citizens who had lent money usuriously or who had tried to justify this practice. No wonder then that in the change of government 1345–6 the new *Signoria* legislated against this form of inquisition. The Republic ceased to prosecute for usury and passed hostile measures such as the suspension of the just price regulations. Moreover, when it funded the public debt at 5 per cent, it did so without any provision, as in the past, for the usury regulations. For the next thirty years or so the government continued to grant its citizens immunity from ecclesiastical courts, and, during the second wave of anti-papalism (this time war had actually broken out) in 1375, the officials of the *monte* "replaced the Church as executors of the wills of manifest usurers." Further restrictions on usurers were removed. Jewish money-lenders were licensed. Communal sanctions against money-lending, which had made interest recoverable at law, were lifted. In the fifteenth century the Jews enjoyed a virtual monopoly of licensed pawnshops or *banchi di pegno* in Florence. From 1437 licences were granted only to Jews. These were the manifest usurers of the councils. They still had some competition, however, from the *banchi a minuto* who made loans secured by jewellery. Much of this was motivated by self-interest. The Florentines had to pay for the cost of the war with the papacy somehow. It had cost them about 2,500,000 gold florins. Wars with the Visconti added another 5,000,000 to the debt. Is it then surprising that here and in Venice (in the War of Chioggia forced loans of 5,000,000 gold ducats had to be raised) and elsewhere in the north, by the early fifteenth century, the application of the Church's legislation on usury was often a matter of political expediency? San Bernardino's comment was short and to the point: "You are all usurers" he told the Florentines. This was not the judgement of a bigoted churchman. Bernardino has been called "the best economist of the Middle Ages" and one who "ranks among the greatest economists of all times." It is true he opposed the foundation of the *Monte delle Doti* at Florence in 1425, by which money was lent to the state and received back fifteen years later with interest as a dowry. On the other hand, in line with the theological principle involved, he supported the receiving of interest on forced loans and he made several exceptions to the strict letter of the law on the ground of *intention*. To the merchants, however, such decisions had become academic ones.

The following example illustrates the operation of the usury laws in the fifteenth century. The account books (*c.* 1415) of Lazzaro Bracci, an Aretine merchant resident in Florence, show that he speculated on the exchange with Venice. He dealt in a large number of loans, but all of a business kind, the borrowers being other bankers and manufacturers. The method used was a type of "dry exchange" known as *cambium ad Venetias*. No bills were transmitted to Venice, but the risk of a change in the market rate beyond the foresight of the lender or borrower was present. The average yield of Bracci's investments was 6.6 per cent. Bracci also had some interest-bearing deposits with the Medici Company, the Medici received from him 300 florins *a discrezione* at 8 per cent. San Antonino (1389–1459) and San Bernardino (1380–1444) had condemned *cambium ad Venetias,* but others, such as Lorenzo di Antonio Ridolfi (1360–1442) approved it with some reservations.

Elsewhere the position was often more openly, if anything, usurious. At Venice loans at 20 per cent against security of land had long been the custom. Luzzatto, in an interesting study, has shown that loans at moderate interest (between 5 and 12 per cent) were regarded as lawful and just, even by the clergy, while the usury laws were directed against immoderate rates. Here usury applied to loans above 12 per cent or loans made with professional usurers outside the state, e.g. with the Tuscan money-lenders at Mestre, and also to concealed contracts, because this could mean excessive rates. Luzzatto's final example was a notarial deed of 9 February 1400, when the struggle against usury was very strong. Giorgio Foscarini says he has received from his dear friend Andrea 200 gold ducats *causa amoris,* and that he will repay *de lucro sive de prode* 5% *in anno.* Thus 5 per cent is regarded as the minimum in such a case of a charitable loan. Luzzatto concludes that "usury can be regarded as the pathological degeneration of a phenomenon of which interest at a variable rate of 5 to 12 per cent was the normal manifestation."

Bruges provides a similar example. The municipal records of the fourteenth and fifteenth centuries list numerous fines collected from persons found guilty of usury in the city court. However, the conditions attaching to the grant of pawnbrokers' licences (for an annual fee) differed in the earlier and later periods. Around 1300 they specifically excluded "manifest" usury and limited the interest to a low figure. But in the fifteenth century false pretences were cast aside and the Lombards were allowed straight usury, "money for money." In Pistoia there had been passed in 1296 the statute "That no public usurer be allowed in the state or diocese of Pistoia," but this, in effect, remained a dead letter. In London, from 1363 onwards, prosecution for usury belonged to the jurisdiction of the mayor and aldermen of the city. In the fifteenth century a special "court of orphanage" had charge of children's portions in estate. From these funds the court formed trust funds from which to lend money at 10 per cent to merchants with sound security. Other companies did the same.

Some commentators have seen in the increasing number of "frauds" proof that the Church's influence on usury was negligible. According to [Gino] Luzzatto the effect of the teaching was slight. This may be true, but the very fact of the fraud proves that the general principle of usury still swayed men's consciences. In the earlier period Gregory IX's decretal *Naviganti,* which condemned sea-loans as usurious, presented a good example of the effect of papal teaching. After 1250 the sea-loan lost favour to the method known as "sea-exchange." Moreover, Luzzatto's criticism neglects to acknowledge the great advances made in the doctrine by the canonists and theologians by restricting the categories to which "usury" applied. These writers had brought the Church's teaching to the point where the taking of moderate interest was regarded as reasonable. The distinction between interest and usury (exorbitant, i.e. unjust, interest) was clear in practice, and it was acted upon, for most of the prosecutions in the later period were for what we would term usury. It is true, neither canonist nor theologian could bring himself to depart radically from the traditional approach that involved such a mass of exemptions and distinctions. This was because they never quite grasped the proper significance of the time-factor in making a loan. As next best, their doctrine of *lucrum cessans, damnum emergens* and *periculum sortis* achieved just that *implicitly.* As to the effect in occult usury,

the reader is reminded of what was said earlier on the importance of the confessional. It is doubtful whether exact elucidation of its importance is possible. But that it had *some* importance was seen by the fact that the general councils tried to enlist the confessional as an instrument of persuasion. . . .

In the fifteenth century the creation of the *montes pietatis,* a sort of municipal, clerical pawnshop "founded for the purpose of relieving the needs of the poor by loans of this kind and thus protecting them against the avarice of usurers," indicates the extent to which the doctrine and practice of usury had changed since the time of Gratian. Ostensibly the *montes* were religious, charitable institutions introduced by the Franciscans in Perugia and Orvieto in 1462. The *montes* collected funds to provide loans to the poor. The subscribers earned no interest, but were offered spiritual rewards. Eventually, to cover "expenses," the poor had to pay interest. Such charges, argued the Dominicans, were usurious because they were levied from the beginning of the loan and were exacted from those who needed the money for the necessities of life. By 1509, despite the conflict of opinion about the lawfulness of interest charged by the *montes,* there were some eighty-seven such institutions in Italy alone. The Dominicans lost their case. Lateran V in the decree *Inter multiplices* sanctioned the *montes* and approved interest with a definition of usury that is qualified and much removed from the simple definition formerly attributed to the Fathers and to Gratian: "Usury means nothing else than gain or profit drawn from the use of a thing that is by its nature sterile, *a profit that is acquired without labour, cost, or risk.* These institutions brought about the virtual disappearance of the public or licensed pawnshops. But occult and unlicensed pawnbrokers continued to thrive, for people often preferred to deal with them rather than with the *montes*.

The Just Price

A like conclusion must be drawn about the just price doctrine in theory and practice. The doctrine from its inception in the twelfth century merely stated that the open or market price was the just one. It allowed the state to regulate prices for the public good. De Roover stressed that success of price controls depended on the municipal authorities: "In the middle ages the implementation of economic policy rested to a large extent, if not exclusively, with the municipal authorities of cities, towns and boroughs. This was especially true of the Italian city states and of the German imperial free cities. Even in England and France the town was the main force in determining economic policy at large. The evidence of municipal records is that the towns tried to impose standards and regulate sale; for example, they encouraged direct sale from producer to consumer to eliminate the middleman and to keep prices down. They took action against individuals and groups who tried to monopolize the market or undercut competitors. Such profits were treated as dishonest and had to be restored. In this way municipal actions reflected the prevailing teaching on the just price.

Direct secular intervention to fix prices occurred, especially in times of severe shortage or for staple products such as wheat, bread, wine, beer, or even to regulate certain types of trade completely. Enactments by the Count of Toulouse in 1181 and 1182 regulated the "practices, prices and wages of butchers, fishmongers, masons and lumber-merchants."

Douai had assizes for a number of basic commodities such as wood, peat, beer, hay, lime and even coffins; the authorities also fixed maximum prices. Some towns introduced "a crude form of rationing," e.g. fixing the price of the loaf, but varying the size. This occurred in France and Germany in the twelfth century. Augsburg varied its "standard loaf" from month to month with the price of wheat. The Spanish theologians advocated free competition as the best means of keeping price control, for price regulation in times of stress seemed ineffective. What it usually led to was a total disappearance of the commodity in question. Maximum price edicts in France and England, in response to the famine of 1315–17, which fixed the price of grain at one-third the then current price, led to a complete withdrawal of grain from the open market. In the end the edicts too were withdrawn. There were, of course, some notable exceptions where state control was highly successful, e.g. the Venetian monopoly of shipping, already cited. In normal times, city authorities could usually fix a "market" price for standard goods. The Mayor of London in the fourteenth century had the duty of setting prices for "ale, beer, red wine, and, after inspection of supplies in the market, for meat and poultry; in the case of fish he [the Mayor] was supposed to inspect each shipload." At certain times the controls were relaxed, e.g. at harvest time, to allow bakers to work without restriction. At other times they were tightened up. After the great storm of 1367 London forbade increases in building trades' wages and prices.

The commonly held belief that the guilds had the *right* to fix the price of their members' products is a fallacy. In fact, and through collusion, they succeeded in doing this, but the doctrine of the just price had been directed at that sort of thing. The municipal authorities legislated to prevent the guilds from usurping this right. Florence in 1293 passed the ordinances of justice and outlawed all price fixing by guilds. Heavy penalties were decreed, but there is no evidence of their being imposed. On the other hand severe fines against workers' guilds or unions were imposed. Scholastic writers and canonists rarely mentioned the guilds, and when they did so, it was to censure them for their monopolistic practices. Unfortunately the scholastic doctrine on monopolies, which was intended to protect the consumer, "led to the paradoxical result of favouring the strong at the expense of the weak and of depriving the masses of workers of all means of collective action." The history of the Italian communes, notably of Venice and Florence, illustrates this very well. In both cities before the 1330s the State prevented any group of capitalists and merchants from gaining supreme control. Subsequently, as in the case of Venice, the State's "military needs, its colonial empire, its shipping and naval industry" led to a breakdown in the balance of interests. Oligarchy eventually came to control the economic and political power in its own interests. Legislation against restrictive guild and trade practices came to smack heavily of political and economic discrimination. In Florence the *Signoria* passed laws in the 1340s and 1350s against the lower guilds, e.g. against the meat-sellers, but sought to extend its own monopolies. In the fifteenth century, state ordinances, such as that of 1440 compelling small farmers to plant five mulberry trees annually for the next decade, served the sectional interests of the silk guild. Nor was it mere coincidence that the leaders of the guild, such as Neri Capponi and Giovanni Guicciardini,

took the lead in waging the war against Florence's rival silk producer, Lucca. Caught between the clash of interests, the lowest-paid workers suffered most. San Antonino accused the Florentine clothiers of paying their employees in kind or in debased coin. But generally the State did nothing to prevent the abuses. [Marvin B.] Becker even concludes that the anti-union attitude of Western Europe and U.S.A. had its origin not in Adam Smith's liberalism and eighteenth-century rationalism, but in medieval scholastic doctrine and statutes of the Italian communes.

By the end of the Middle Ages, canonistic teaching on monopolies and just price had little practical effect. The doctrines did, however, perform a useful function by standing for those ideals that have constantly "to be recalled to the minds of men because they have not been fulfilled." The clergy no longer had much influence in municipal affairs. Self-interest occasionally worked wonders: Richental's *Chronicle of Constance* describes how "envoys of the Pope, the King and other lords appeared before the town council of Constance, and said they were paying too dear for lodgings and that the price of all victuals was unfairly reckoned. So the council appointed delegates to meet with them, and they made the following ordinance . . ." This fixed prices until, with normal supplies available, "the prices of everything diminished." But these incidents were exceptions. The growth of municipal government led to a policy of exclusion of clerics from public office and from the affairs of the communes. In Germany, which in the thirteenth century saw the rise of 400 new towns, the municipalities took control of appointing their own priests and also of church property. With these changes there passed also responsi-

JOHN GILCHRIST

bility and control of charitable works, as we shall see.

Charity and the Poor

With the question of the medieval teaching on charity and the poor we are on surer ground. In the primitive Church episcopal and private charity sufficed. The early Christians even widened the scope of relief to include non-Christians and the able-bodied. There were limits, of course. Thus the able-bodied had to earn their keep after two or three days' free aid. The seeds of the later discriminatory theory of the canonists were being sown. With the economic revolution of the tenth century onwards, there emerged an organized system of parochial relief, which, down to about 1300, was effective and usually sufficient. After 1300 its effectiveness declined only slightly, but it was no longer sufficient. The canonistic teaching on charity and the uses of wealth developed a highly sophisticated theory of responsibility towards the poor. Especially, the able-bodied were not encouraged to be idle. Secular legislation and general practice reflected the canonistic doctrine. In England the Statute of Cambridge of 1388 introduced the distinction between the able-bodied and the sick. London merchants, according to Sylvia Thrupp, seemed to feel "reluctant to oppress the poor . . . Pity, however, was only for the industrious poor, not for the astute hangers-on." Unfortunately, by this time, the medieval poor law had become inadequate and frustrated. The new social and economic factors produced large numbers of vagrant, unemployed and able-bodied workers. Increasingly the gap between rich and poor widened, and, correspondingly, the sense of responsibility of one class towards the other lessened.

Florence provides a good example of the unequal distribution of wealth from about 1350 onwards. The *Signoria* financed its wars by special forced loans that earned interest at a nominal 5 per cent, but in fact at 15 per cent. Payment of the interest was usually met by a tax on consumables, which therefore fell disproportionately on the lesser guildsmen and workers. The attractive rate of interest offered by the *monte* created further economic difficulties, for some investors withdrew from commercial enterprises and put their money into war loans. This affected industrial development.

Amidst poverty, reigned plenty. The following text from Pius II's *Commentaries* needs no comment:

Francesco Sforza . . . sent the Pope three very fat steers which had been fed on turnips and were used to being washed with warm water, combed every day, and bedded on clean straw. . . . All liked the meat so much that they vowed they had never tasted anything sweeter, but it was not bought cheaply, for those who brought the oxen were presented with 100 gold ducats.

Gradually there emerged a different attitude towards poverty. It ceased to be a misfortune, a blessing of Providence, a virtue extolled by Christ in the Sermon on the Mount. It took on a more modern aspect of a crime, "an assault by the poor upon society itself." The poor found refuge in heresies and obscurantist movements that only caused the church authorities to apply the law more strictly. They also found refuge in periodic uprisings that demonstrated social and political inarticulateness. For the workers, although they carried heavy tax burdens, were without guilds and therefore without real access to the then accepted means of political expression and social reform. For these needs the canonists did nothing, although their doctrines continued into the sixteenth century to serve as a basis for systems of poor relief. Thus in England the State replaced the Church as the directing body, but the medieval parish organization on which the poor law was based lasted till the nineteenth century.

Monastic charity played no great part in these developments. In the early Church the problem of relief of the poor, e.g. at Rome, fell to the *diaconiae,* a kind of charitable centre, which existed apart from the monasteries. Eventually, when the *diaconiae* lost their original charitable functions in the ninth century, there succeeded the efforts of the bishop and diocesan clergy. Neither the black nor the white monks were so located that they could attend to the needs of the new poor that came with the economic expansion. The lay religious Orders in their inception from Robert de Arbrisselles (d. 1117) to Francis of Assisi (d. 1226) had a great sympathy with the poor, but they too became institutionalized and involved in the struggle to compete with other religious and secular clergy.

Studies of individual monasteries confirm that, generally, the monks were not over-liberal in their alms-giving. In the later Middle Ages the allocations virtually ceased. An analysis of the account-books of Canterbury cathedral priory for the period 1284–1373 shows that only 0.52 per cent of the almoner's income went to the poor, plus some gifts of food and clothing. Most of the revenue went to the upkeep of the almoner's own large household or to maintain the *pauperes Dei,* i.e. fellow monks. Benedictine abbeys were not intended as hospitals for the sick. A General Chapter held at Lérins in 1351 decreed that "no sick, no lame or weakly constituted, no bastard or non-Catholics shall enter without the express consent of the abbot, and never younger than fourteen."

Contrasted with the monks, popes, princes and other secular and spiritual leaders spent a good percentage of their income on alms. King John of England . . . spent about 6 per cent of his income on charity; Pope John XXII's gifts represented 7.16 per cent of his total expenditure. Eugenius IV, when he put the Hospital of the Holy Spirit in Rome back into repair, revived the arch-confraternity that supported it and promised an annual gift. His cardinals followed suit. There are over thirty extant bulls of Eugenius IV in which he aided French hospitals. Most communes contributed to the support of the city's hospitals and other charitable institutions. Orvieto exempted church property from taxation and gave varying sums of money to the hospitals.

One matter, however, in which the friars displayed initiative was in the provision of the *montes pietatis.* This did something to solve one of the gravest social problems of the Middle Ages, namely, the lack of consumer credit for the workers. But, unwittingly, the theorists had done much to create and aggravate that problem. They failed to realize that "charitable" loans were not a satisfactory solution to the problem of consumer credit. The rise of the pawnbroker and petty money-lender in the earlier period at least reflected the need for their services. But the Church in seeking to prevent high rates of interest by concentrating on the manifest usurers—the pawnbrokers, in effect—and driving them out of business, only succeeded in making such loans more risky and therefore subject to an even higher rate of interest. The canonists and theologians overlooked the fact that the lender temporarily transferred his purchasing power to the borrower, and hence his capacity to enjoy the fruits of his labour. The debtors were thereby enabled to anticipate future earnings, even if they did so by consuming the loan. The professional pawnbrokers performed a service that called for a proper recognition. Here alone is where the Church's usury laws had their greatest effect, and it was a moral and social rather than an economic disaster that resulted. For the masses blamed the Church for their plight, and the *montes pietatis* came too late to save the Church in regions other than in Italy and Spain, where they were most widespread.

In general, the Church's influence on economic activity both as a temporal power and as a spiritual body with teaching powers was a positive one during the period of economic expansion *c.* 1000–*c.* 1300. In the subsequent economic decline the Church was too divided by internal schism and dissension, and challenged externally by the rising national states, to keep pace with the changing form of society. Lateran V illustrates the poverty of reform ideas on the eve of the Reformation. The Reformation came and the initiative passed to the State.

GEORGE GORDON COULTON (1858–1947) was a
pioneer in the writing of medieval social history. His
work did much to weaken the influence of his romantic
contemporaries who portrayed medieval life in an
idyllic manner. *The Medieval Scene* consists of eleven
essays on various aspects of medieval life. In these
Coulton tries to bring his readers to an understanding
of the real Middle Ages.*

George Gordon Coulton

The Peasants' Search for Salvation

This matter of Just Price and Usury
was worth dwelling upon at some length,
not only for its intrinsic interest, but
also because that department of social
life in the Middle Ages is only one of
many in which we shall stray very far
from historical truth if we imagine that
the medieval hierarchy and the Universities, or even the whole body of clergy,
can by themselves give us an adequate
conception of the average man's ideas.
For the average man, unconsciously yet
very truly, was in effect dictating to his
betters, even in regions where a superficial view regards him only as submitting
to dictation. Many of the most influential
medieval doctrines (as, for example, its
lurid eschatology) had in fact grown up
from below. The schoolmen did indeed
defend these tenets with every reinforce-
ment of logical subtlety, but with regard
to the tenets themselves they had no
original choice. With all St Thomas's
originality in many directions, he was
obliged in many others to start from
premises inherited from past generations
during which the hierarchy had gradually
adopted and consecrated popular beliefs.
The same is true even of some among the
most important Church ceremonies and
holy-days. Of all the saints in the Roman
Calendar, probably 75 per cent at least
owe their position to popular choice,
not only before Alexander III (d. 1181)
reserved canonisation for Popes alone
but before even the earlier stage at which

*From George Gordon Coulton, *The Medieval Scene* (London: Cambridge University Press, 1959), pp.
151–163. Footnotes omitted.

97

the diocesan bishop had possessed similar powers. Again, what is now one of the most striking red-letter-days of the Roman Church, that of Corpus Christi, was due almost entirely to an enthusiastic girl and a young unlearned priest. Their suggestion was taken up by the then archdeacon of Liège, destined afterwards to become Urban IV. In 1246 the Bishop of Liège ordered the festival to be kept in his diocese; and in 1264 Urban, as Pope, published a bull in its favour. Yet even about 1300 the feast was not universally recognised; and it was Clement V (d. 1314) and John XXII (d. 1334) whose decrees did most to render it universal. But demand creates supply; simple minds demanded simple solutions of the most complex problems of life, and thus the official answers were dictated, to some real extent, by the intellectual limitations of the questioners. The lofty abstractions of Paulinism or of the Johannine writings could scarcely have worn through the Dark Ages without a heavy admixture of some such alloy. For unity's sake, Church teachers were compelled to be all things to all men, even at the expense of taking, here and there, a permanent tinge from that to which they had condescended. And this idea of unity outlasted the Dark Ages; it may even be said to have attained to its most definite expression only when these were past, and when the world had settled down into the comparative stability of the thirteenth century. By that time, two generations of great thinkers had toiled to weave the accepted beliefs of their day into one harmonious philosophic whole; and then came the temptation to stiffen in self-satisfied repose. A modern Scholastic can boast, with no more than pardonable exaggeration: "The thirteenth century believed that it had realised a state of stable equilibrium; and [men's] extraordinary opti-

mism led them to believe that they had arrived at a state close to perfection." In so far, therefore, as medieval thought can be described with any approach to truth in a single sentence, it may perhaps be characterised as a struggle for unity; a worship of unity which amounted almost to idolatry. We may apply to the Middle Ages the half-true epigram which reflects one side of the French Revolution: "Be my brother, or I kill thee!" With the same half-truth we may put into the mouth of a medieval thinker: "Be at unity with me, or be burned!" We ourselves are too ready, perhaps, to take divergencies for granted and even to make a merit of them. But the passion for outward unity was one of the main forces in medieval reconstruction; it was the most obvious rallying point in Church and State. The mystic has been admirably defined by Dr McTaggart as one who feels a greater unity in the universe than that which is recognised in ordinary experience, and who believes that he can become conscious of this unity in some more direct way than in that of ordinary discursive thought. It would seem, therefore, that all constructive ideas must have a strong element of mysticism; and this is one justification of the modern revived interest in the Middle Ages. We may hold that there is more real unity in modern society, beneath its outward divergencies; and yet we may feel that we have something real to learn from those who strove harder than we do for outward unity. At any rate, for them it was one of the necessities of their position; here, for many centuries, seemed the only escape from anarchy in State or in Church.

We have here only the specially strong and enduring manifestation of a phenomenon which is common elsewhere in history. Rightly enough, men will catch at any escape from anarchy. If the *ancien régime* lasted so long, it was because the only alternatives were the tyranny of a squirearchy, or else the helpless confusion of a populace which lacked both leaders and political experience. Napoleon, again, was rightly welcomed as the alternative to a mob-rule which had still so much political sense to learn before it could succeed. Just as the peasants of the Dark Ages were glad, on the whole, to rally round the nearest fighting man, and even commit their liberties to him, so they were quite content to rally round the priest. The Church, with very little question, with its strong sense of social solidarity, gave them neighbourly and religious warmth; her teaching and example, even when all necessary deductions have been made, were definitely on the side of brotherhood. It is true that her higher speculations were mostly above the head of the average man; but even here there was some real infiltration, and we find not infrequent examples of high mystical enthusiasm among the unlearned. Her ordinary ceremonies, and many of her beliefs, since they had sprung to so great an extent from the multitude, were therefore acceptable and comfortable to the multitude. It is noteworthy that, in the Dark Ages, heresy seems to have been always unpopular; heretics were often lynched, and sometimes, apparently, not even by priestly initiative. Anything rather than anarchy; and the average man, quite apart from his uncultured dislike of anything strange and perplexing, realised dimly that these dissentients were not strong enough, either numerically or individually, to rebuild Church or State if either were destroyed.

But civilisation advanced and knowledge increased; then the average man became more thoughtful, and therefore more critical of an institution which had not sufficient elasticity to keep pace with the general growth of society. One cause of strength in the Scholastic doctrine was that it often rested on foundations of popular belief; but, in its very completeness, in the perfection and calculated imperishability of its structure, it was apt to find itself finally in conflict with popular feeling, which, in its very nature, is changeable and slowly progressive. Nothing can be more dangerous than the belief that we have arrived at a state close to perfection. There is good common sense at the bottom of Lord Balfour's cynical answer to the friend who showed him the Woolworth Building in New York and extolled it at the same time as fireproof from top to bottom—"What a pity!" At all times, the severest test of a half-truth is that a philosopher should pursue it to its logical consequences. Given the premises which were accepted by hierarchy and laity alike, Aquinas was impeccably logical in proving that it is the Christian's duty to remove obstinate nonconformists at any cost, even at that of the stake. But to lynch in the heat of passion is one thing, to kill by implacable logic is another; and the Inquisition was never popular, even among men whose ancestors had with their own hands cast the heretic into an extemporised bonfire. Its unpopularity increased when it became evident how definitely it was nourished by the fines and confiscations imposed upon rich heretics; and, again, how fatally it lent itself (as in the cases of the Templars and Joan of Arc) to purely political purposes. Moreover, the most unimpeachably orthodox scholars sometimes recognised that one of the main tenets of the heretics, their objection to oaths, could scarcely be condemned in the face of Christ's plain words. Therefore the cruelties and injustices of the Inquisition—very great, even when we have stripped the story of all exaggerations—go far to account for such an utterance as we find recorded against a heretic of Toulouse in 1347: "This man Peter said also that, if he could hold that god who, of a thousand men whom he had made, saved one and damned all the rest, then he would tear and rend him with tooth and nail as a traitor, and would brand him as false and traitorous, and would spit in his face." The wave of popular mysticism which seems to have begun in Dominican circles on the upper Rhine at the end of the thirteenth century, and thence to have spread by the trade route to the lower Rhine and England, showed, among other manifestations, a strong tendency to escape from the cruel theology which, as very commonly preached and understood, is set forth without exaggeration in this man Peter's words. This humanitarian effort is noticeable in three of Chaucer's contemporaries, Rulman Merswin of Strassburg, Juliana the anchoress of Norwich, and the author (or authors) of *Piers Plowman.*

This last-mentioned poem serves better than any other medieval document as text for a disquisition on the mind of ordinary men in the later Middle Ages. Nobody, it is true, can understand medieval life who has not read Dante's *Divine Comedy;* but *Piers Plowman* is an even better index to the mind of the multitude. In that poem we have a picture of all classes, including the very poorest, as reflected in the daily thoughts of educated fourteenth-century Londoners at their best. The very incoherence of the book is in this sense one of its main merits; the author is always thinking aloud; he reveals all his moods, untroubled by fear of self-contradiction; he mirrors faithfully the medley of ordinary human thought. He shows us one characteristic which ran through the whole Middle Ages and survived, for instance, with so many

other medieval factors, in societies like that of the *ancien régime.* This is the emphasis on privilege side by side with law, and, it may almost be said, on privilege even above law—an emphasis which is not really contradicted, but rather strengthened, by those who would remind us that medieval privileges were part of medieval law. Radical as the author is in politics and in religion, he accepts the distinction of classes as God-ordained. Not that the compartments are absolutely water-tight, but no interchange is contemplated under normal conditions; he looks upon it as a social scandal that bondmen's bairns should be made bishops and that soap-sellers or their sons should be knighted. As a matter of fact, very few such cases as the former are recorded in all the range of medieval history; hence, no doubt, the greater scandal to the average thinker. There was much else to exercise this fourteenth-century Londoner's mind. The Hundred Years' War and the Black Death, he sees, have shaken society to its foundations. At one extreme are ex-soldiers and labourers taking advantage of the plague to claim higher wages and idler days, though St Paul wrote, "he that will not work, neither shall he eat." At the other, we have a boy-king led by evil counsellors; a nobility and a squirearchy against whose oppressions Peace formally petitions to Parliament in the name of the poor; and Commons who would willingly seize the government into their own hands, if only they dared to bell the cat. With all this social disorder the author has little sympathy, though he is poor himself, living from hand to mouth, and men take him for a madman because he will not make obeisance to great folk in office or in silks and furs. One of his main themes is this of the dignity of honest poverty and work. Peter the Ploughman (he says) can lead us as straight to heaven as the parish priest himself; yet this, after all, must be by the old and narrow way: "they that have done good shall go into eternal life, and they that have done evil into everlasting fire." Meanwhile, it is a disjointed world through which we have to find our way from the cradle to the grave. Money rules everything; the man who can bribe is the man who grows to greatness; justice is bought and sold; the great town houses are built and inhabited by wholesale dealers in rotten stuff, who "poison privily and oft the poor people that parcelmeal buyen." Life is a jostle for worldly success; "the most part of this people that passeth on this earth, of other heaven than here hold they no tale."

Yet our author's own faith is unshaken; he steadily trusts the larger hope. Not that he sees his way everywhere so clearly; the whole book is full of theological problems which he attacks yet cannot solve. Nor can the parish priest solve them for him; the friar, again, for all his fat red face and bold verbosity, leaves him equally puzzled; and the professional pilgrim, when the real pinch comes, proves a broken reed. All of us, as loyal church-folk, wish to believe in papal indulgences; yet how can we reconcile these with the supreme value of good works? How can we reconcile predestination with free will? Why should posterity suffer for Adam's sin? Our poet himself grapples reverently with these problems, but he tells us of great folk at whose high table the after-dinner discussions are anything but reverent

At meat in their mirthës, when minstrels be still then tell they of the trinity a tale or twain, and bring forth a bold reason, and take Bernard to witness. Thus they drivel at their dais, the deity to know, And gnaw on God with the gorge, when their gut is full. . . .
I have heard high men eating at table carping, as they clerkës were, of Christ and

of His mights, And lay faults upon the Father that formëd us all. . . . Why would our Saviour suffer such a worm in his bliss, That beguiled the woman, and the man after, Through which wiles and wordes they wenten to hell? . . . Why should we that now be, for the works of Adam Rot or suffer torment? reason would it never! Such motives they move, these masters in their glory, And maken men to misbelieve that muse much on their words.

But all these uncertainties, from which no thinking man can escape in any age, drive our poet more and more inward into the sanctuary of his own soul. For himself, he is sure of a few fundamental things. Truth is paramount, Truth is God Almighty. But Truth is not in mere intellectuality; to learn is "Do-Well"; to teach is "Do-Better"; "Do-Best" is to love. Heaven is not for the wise, as men count wisdom, but for the good. Solomon the wise is probably now in hell; yet many poor simple folk "pierce with a paternoster the palace of heaven." And, above all, when we have no other stay, let us contemplate the life and work of Christ. Christ died, Christ reigns, and we, if we fight the good fight, shall reign with him; that is the main theme for all the last cantos of this poem. Still, "fight" is the word. True, Christ is in heaven; true, again, that here on earth we have the Pope, Christ's vicar through Peter; but the history of the Church has been a sad story, for Satan had soon crept in after the Ascension, and had "coloured things so quaintly" that honest folk, ever since, have scarce known what to think. In this England of Chaucer's day the mass of Christians are described as a flock of shepherdless sheep; they "blustered forth as beasts over banks and hills, till late was and long." The professional pilgrim proved quite helpless when these folk, weary of the well-worn shrines, asked the way to a new saint, to Saint Truth; to that appeal he could only shake his head;

that is a saint unknown to the Pilgrims' Way. And, now that Antichrist is preparing another and fiercer attack upon Christ's folk, who have entrenched themselves as best they can within the fold of Holy Church, it is the clergy themselves who become the worst traitors; first the priests, and then the friars. Then the enemy comes on more fiercely: where is Conscience, who has been set to keep the gate of Holy Church? "He lieth and dreameth," said Peace, "and so do many other; The Friar with his physic this folk hath enchanted, And plastered them so easily, they dread no sin."

Here, within seven lines of the end of the poem, there seems no room for a hopeful conclusion. Yet the author's personal religion is proof against all shocks of disillusion and disappointment; he is "one of those rare thinkers who fight fiercely for moderate ideas, and employ all the resources of a fiery soul in support of common sense" (Jusserand). Christ reigns still; if His fold is thus taken by storm, then let us shake the dust of it from our feet and go forth as solitary pilgrims, "as wide as all the world lasteth," in search of the Christ that is to be:

"By Christ!" (quoth Conscience then) "I will become a pilgrim
And walken, as wide as all the worldë lasteth
To seek Piers the Plowman, that Pride may be destroyed,
And that friars may find their guerdon who flatter for gain
And counterplead me, Conscience. Now, Nature me avenge,
And send me good hap and heal, till I have Piers the Plowman!"
And then he groaned after grace, and I gan awake.

The whole book, supported as it is by multitudinous indications from elsewhere, shows us the growth of a simple mystic religion among the people. And this, side by side with the well-known Renaissance of learning among scholars, nobles and merchants, with a general and growing impatience of moral abuses, and with concurrent economic causes, worked for the change from the medieval to the modern mind. Great churchmen, for generations past, had pointed out clearly that, unless means could be found for reforming the Church from top to bottom—*Reformation in Head and members* became the regular cry—from the Roman court down to the ordinary priest and his parishioners—then revolution could not be avoided. That revolution had been as long foreseen as the French Revolution of 1789; and at last the unavoidable thing came. Like all other revolutions, it brought havoc and unsettlement; but, for good and for evil, it made modern Europe. Intolerance was still the rule for many generations, and it may be argued with some appearance of truth that this intolerance was equally violent among all the contending parties; yet, in the long run, these party contentions have forced tolerance even upon the most unwilling minds. Facts have proved, what reason was proving only slowly and fitfully, that no party can have any hope of exterminating the other, and therefore that all must arrange themselves so as to live together in this world of bewilderingly various tastes and ideas In this matter of toleration, one of the most important for human progress, the world had turned away, to all appearance for ever, from the mind that was natural to medieval Europe.

Few historians of culture have been adequate in both transmitting a convincing portrait of their subject and at the same time earning the respect of professionals for the standards of their scholarship. JOHAN HUIZINGA (1872–1945) was one such scholar, and *The Waning of the Middle Ages* is a model which would be difficult to surpass. Huizinga's use and command of so very many genres of historical source material both written and nonwritten cannot fail to impress even his most learned readers.*

Johan Huizinga

The Image of Religion

Towards the end of the Middle Ages two factors dominate religious life: the extreme saturation of the religious atmosphere, and a marked tendency of thought to embody itself in images.

Individual and social life, in all their manifestations, are imbued with the conceptions of faith. There is not an object nor an action, however trivial, that is not constantly correlated with Christ or salvation. All thinking tends to religious interpretation of individual things; there is an enormous unfolding of religion in daily life. This spiritual wakefulness, however, results in a dangerous state of tension, for the presupposed transcendental feelings are sometimes dormant,

and whenever this is the case, all that is meant to stimulate spiritual consciousness is reduced to appalling commonplace profanity, to a startling worldliness in other-worldly guise. Only saints are capable of an attitude of mind in which the transcendental faculties are never in abeyance.

The spirit of the Middle Ages, still plastic and naïve, longs to give concrete shape to every conception. Every thought seeks expression in an image, but in this image it solidifies and becomes rigid. By this tendency to embodiment in visible forms all holy concepts are constantly exposed to the danger of hardening into mere externalism. For in assuming a

*From Johan Huizinga, *The Waning of the Middle Ages* (New York: St. Martin's Press, 1959), pp. 151–177. Reprinted by permission of Edward Arnold (Publishers), Ltd., and St. Martin's Press. Where foreign-language quotations are given in the text in the original with translations in English in footnotes, the foreign-language quotations have been omitted and the translations placed in the text. Other footnotes have been omitted.

definite figurative shape thought loses its ethereal and vague qualities, and pious feeling is apt to resolve itself in the image.

Even in the case of a sublime mystic, like Henry Suso, the craving for hallowing every action of daily life verges in our eyes on the ridiculous. He is sublime when, following the usages of profane love, he celebrates New Year's Day and May Day by offering a wreath and a song to his betrothed, Eternal Wisdom, or when, out of reverence for the Holy Virgin, he renders homage to all womankind and walks in the mud to let a beggar woman pass. But what are we to think of what follows? At table Suso eats three-quarters of an apple in the name of the Trinity and the remaining quarter in commemoration of "the love with which the heavenly Mother gave her tender child Jesus an apple to eat"; and for this reason he eats the last quarter with the paring, as little boys do not peel their apples. After Christmas he does not eat it, for then the infant Jesus was too young to eat apples. He drinks in five draughts because of the five wounds of the Lord, but as blood and water flowed from the side of Christ, he takes his last draught twice. This is, indeed, pushing the sanctification of life to extremes.

In so far as it concerns individual piety, this tendency to apply religious conceptions to all things and at all times is a deep source of saintly life. As a cultural phenomenon this same tendency harbours grave dangers. Religion penetrating all relations in life means a constant blending of the spheres of holy and of profane thought. Holy things will become too common to be deeply felt. The endless growth of observances, images, religious interpretations, signifies an augmentation in quantity at which serious divines grew alarmed, as they feared the quality would deteriorate proportionately. The warning which we find recurring in all reformist writings of the time of the schism and of the councils is—the Church is being overloaded.

Pierre d'Ailly, in condemning the novelties which were incessantly introduced into the liturgy and the sphere of belief, is less concerned about the piety of their character than about the steady increase itself. The signs of the ever-ready divine grace multiplied endlessly; a host of special benedictions sprang up side by side with the sacraments; in addition to relics we find amulets; the bizarre gallery of saints became ever more numerous and variegated. However emphatically divines insisted upon the difference between sacraments and *sacramentalia,* the people would still confound them. Gerson tells how he met a man at Auxerre, who maintained that All Fools' Day was as sacred as the day of the Virgin's Conception. Nicolas de Clemanges wrote a treatise, *De novis festivitatibus non instituendis,* in which he denounced the apocryphal nature of some among these new institutions. Pierre d'Ailly, in *De Reformatione,* deplores the ever-increasing number of churches, of festivals, of saints, of holydays; he protests against the multitude of images and paintings, the prolixity of the Service, against the introduction of new hymns and prayers, against the augmentation of vigils and fasts. In short, what alarms him is the evil of superfluity.

There are too many religious orders, says d'Ailly, and this leads to a diversity of usages, to exclusiveness and rivalry, to pride and vanity. In particular he desired to impose restrictions on the mendicant orders, whose social utility he questions: they live to the detriment of the inmates of leper houses and hospitals, and other really poor and wretched people, who are truly entitled to beg *(ac aliis vere pauperibus et miserabilibus indigentibus quibus convenit jus et versus titulus mendicandi).* Let the sellers of indulgences be banished from the Church, which they soil with their lives and make ridiculous. Convents are built on all sides, but sufficient funds are lacking. Where is this to lead?

Pierre d'Ailly does not question the holy and pious character of all these practices in themselves, he only deplores their endless multiplication; he sees the Church weighed down under the load of particulars.

Religious customs tended to multiply in an almost mechanical way. A special office was instituted for every detail of the worship of the Virgin Mary. There were particular masses, afterwards abolished by the Church, in honour of the piety of Mary, of her seven sorrows, of all her festivals taken collectively, of her sisters—the two other Marys—of the archangel Gabriel, of all the saints of our Lord's genealogy. A curious example of this spontaneous accretion of religious usage is found in the weekly observance of Innocents' Day. The 28th of December, the day of the massacre at Bethlehem, was taken to be ill-omened. This belief was the origin of a custom, widely spread during the fifteenth century, of considering as a black-letter day, all the year through, the day of the week on which the preceding Innocents' Day fell. Consequently, there was one day in every week on which people abstained from setting out upon a journey and beginning a new task, and this day was called Innocents' Day, like the festival itself. Louis XI observed this usage scrupulously. The coronation of Edward IV of England was repeated, as it had taken place on a Sunday, because the 28th of December of the previous year had been a Sunday too. René de Lorraine had to give up his plan of fighting a battle on the 17th of October, 1476, as his lansquenets refused to encounter the enemy "on Innocents' Day."

This belief, of which we find some traces appearing in England as late as the eighteenth century, called forth a treatise from Gerson against superstition in general. His penetrating mind had realized some of the danger with which these excrescences of the creed menaced the purity of religious thought. He was aware of their psychological basis; according to him, these beliefs proceed *ex sola hominum phantasiatione et melancholica imaginatione;* it is a disorder of the imagination caused by some lesion of the brain, which in its turn is due to diabolic illusions.

The Church was constantly on her guard lest dogmatic truth should be confounded with this mass of facile beliefs, and lest the exuberance of popular fancy should degrade God. But was she able to stand against this strong need of giving a concrete form to all the emotions accompanying religious thought? It was an irresistible tendency to reduce the infinite to the finite, to disintegrate all mystery. The highest mysteries of the creed became covered with a crust of superficial piety. Even the profound faith in the eucharist expands into childish beliefs—for instance, that one cannot go blind or have a stroke of apoplexy on a day on which one has heard mass, or that one does not grow older during the time spent in attending mass. While herself offering so much food to the popular imagination, the Church could not claim to keep that imagination within the limits of a healthy and vigorous piety.

In this respect the case of Gerson is characteristic. He composed a treatise, *Contra vanam curiositatem,* by which he means the spirit of research which desires to scrutinize the secrets of nature. But whilst protesting against it, he himself becomes guilty of a curiosity which to us seems out of place and deplorable. Gerson was the great promoter of the adoration of Saint Joseph. His veneration for this saint makes him desirous of learning all that concerns him. He routs out all particulars of the married life of Joseph: his continence, his age, the way in which he learned of the Virgin's pregnancy. He is indignant at the caricature of a drudging and ridiculous Joseph, which the arts were inclined to make of him. In another passage Gerson indulges in a speculation on the bodily constitution of Saint John the Baptist: *Semen igitur materiale ex qua corpus compaginandum erat, nec durum nimis nec rursus fluidum abundantius fruit.* [1]

Whether the Virgin had taken an active part in the supernatural conception, or, again, whether the body of Christ would have decomposed, if it had not been for the resurrection, were what the popular preacher Olivier Maillard called "beautiful theological questions" to discuss before his auditors. The mixture of theological and embryological speculation to which the controversy about the immaculate conception of the Virgin gave rise shocked the minds of that period so little that grave divines did not scruple to treat the subject from the pulpit.

This familiarity with sacred things is, on the one hand, a sign of deep and ingenuous faith; on the other, it entails irreverence whenever mental contact with the infinite fails. Curiosity, ingenuous though it be, leads to profanation. In the fifteenth century people used to keep statuettes of the Virgin, of which the body opened and showed the Trinity

within. The inventory of the treasure of the dukes of Burgundy makes mention of one made of gold inlaid with gems. Gerson saw one in the Carmelite monastery at Paris; he blames the brethren for it, not, however, because such a coarse picture of the miracle shocked him as irreverent, but because of the heresy of representing the Trinity as the fruit of Mary.

All life was saturated with religion to such an extent that the people were in constant danger of losing sight of the distinction between things spiritual and things temporal. If, on the one hand, all details of ordinary life may be raised to a sacred level, on the other hand, all that is holy sinks to the commonplace by the fact of being blended with everyday life. In the Middle Ages the demarcation of the sphere of religious thought and that of worldly concerns was nearly obliterated. It occasionally happened that indulgences figured among the prizes of a lottery. When a prince was making a solemn entry, the altars at the corners of the streets, loaded with the precious reliquaries of the town and served by prelates, might be seen alternating with dumb shows of pagan goddesses or comic allegories.

Nothing is more characteristic in this respect than the fact of there being hardly any difference between the musical character of profane and sacred melodies. Till late in the sixteenth century profane melodies might be used indiscriminately for sacred use, and sacred for profane. It is notorious that Guillaume Dufay and others composed masses to the theme of love-songs, such as "So much I enjoy myself," "If my face is pale," "The armed man."

There was a constant interchange of religious and profane terms. No one felt offended by hearing the Day of

---

[1] "Therefore the seed in its material nature from which the body was made was neither too solid nor was it too fluid.—B. S. B.

Judgment compared to a settling of accounts, as in the verses formerly written over the door of the audit office at Lille.

Then to the sound of the trumpet God shall open His general and grand audit office.

A tournament, on the other hand, is called "des armes grantdisime pardon" (the great indulgence conferred by arms) as if it were a pilgrimage. By a chance coincidence the words *mysterium* and *ministerium* were blended in French into the form "mistère," and this homonymy must have helped to efface the true sense of the word "mystery" in everyday parlance, because even the most commonplace things might be called "mistère."

While religious symbolism represented the realities of nature and history as symbols or emblems of salvation, on the other hand religious metaphors were borrowed to express profane sentiments. People in the Middle Ages, standing in awe of royalty, do not shrink from using the language of adoration in praising princes. In the lawsuit about the murder of Louis of Orléans, the counsel for the defence makes the shade of the duke say to his son: "Look at my wounds and observe that *five* of them are particularly cruel and mortal." The bishop of Chalons, Jean Germain, in his *Liber de virtutibus Philippi ducis Burgundiae,* in his turn does not scruple to compare the victim of Montereau to the Lamb. The Emperor Frederick III, when sending his son Maximilian to the Low Countries to marry Mary of Burgundy, is compared by Molinet to God the Father. The same author makes the people of Brussels say, when they wept with tenderness on seeing the emperor entering their town with Maximilian and Philip le Beau: "Behold the image of the Trinity, the Father, the Son and the Holy Ghost." He offers a wreath of flowers to Mary of Burgundy,

a worthy image of Our Lady, "Save the virginity." "Not that I want to deify princes."

Although we may consider such formulae of adulation empty phrases, they show none the less the depreciation of sacred imagery resulting from its hackneyed use. We can hardly blame a court poet, when Gerson himself ascribes to the royal auditors of his sermons guardian angels of a higher rank in the celestial hierarchy than those of other men.

The step from familiarity to irreverence is taken when religious terms are applied to erotic relations. The subject has been dealt with above. The author of the *Quinze Joyes de Mariage* chose his title to accord with the joys of the Virgin. The defender of the *Roman de la Rose* used sacred terms to designate the *partes corporis inhonestas et peccata immunda atque turpia.* No instance of this dangerous association of religious with amatory sentiments could be more striking than the Madonna ascribed to Fouquet, making part of a diptych which was formerly preserved at Melun and is now partly at Antwerp and partly at Berlin; Antwerp possessing the Madonna and Berlin the panel representing the donor, Etienne Chevalier, the king's treasurer, together with Saint Stephen. In the seventeenth century Denis Godefroy noted down a tradition, then already old, according to which the Madonna had the features of Agnès Sorel, the royal mistress, for whom Chevalier felt a passion that he did not trouble to conceal. However this may be, the Madonna is, in fact, represented here according to the canons of contemporary fashion: there is the bulging shaven forehead, the rounded breasts, placed high and wide apart, the high and slender waist. The bizarre inscrutable expression of the Madonna's face, the red and blue cherubim surrounding her, all contribute to give this painting an air of decadent impiety in spite of the stalwart figure of the donor. Godefroy observed on the large frame of blue velvet E's done in pearls linked by love-knots of gold and silver thread. There is a flavour of blasphemous boldness about the whole, unsurpassed by any artist of the Renaissance.

The irreverence of daily religious practice was almost unbounded. Choristers, when chanting mass, did not scruple to sing the words of the profane songs that had served as a theme for the composition: "Kiss me," "Red noses."

A startling piece of impudence is recorded of the father of the Frisian humanist Rodolph, Agricola, who received news that his concubine had given birth to a son on the very day when he was elected abbot. "To-day I have twice become a father. God's blessing on it!" said he.

At the end of the fourteenth century people took the increasing irreverence to be an evil of recent date, which, indeed, is a common phenomenon at all times. Deschamps deplores it in the following lines:

In bygone times people used to be Gentle in church, On their knees in humility Close beside the altar, With meekly uncovered head, But at present, like beasts, They too often come to the altar With hood and hat on their heads.

On festal days, says Nicolas de Clemanges, few people go to mass. They do not stay till the end, and are content with touching the holy water, bowing before Our Lady, or kissing the image of some saint. If they wait for the elevation of the Host, they pride themselves upon it, as if they had conferred a benefit on Christ. At matins and vespers the priest and his assistant are the only persons present. The squire of the village makes the priest wait to begin mass till he and his wife have risen and dressed. The most sacred festivals, even Christmas night, says Gerson, are passed in debauchery, playing at cards, swearing and blaspheming. When the people are admonished, they plead the example of the nobility and the clergy, who behave in like manner with impunity. Vigils likewise, says Clemanges, are kept with lascivious songs and dances, even in church; priests set the example by dicing as they watch. It may be said that moralists paint things in too dark colours; but in the accounts of Strassburg we find a yearly gift of 1,100 litres of wine granted by the council to those who "watched in prayer" in church during the night of Saint Adolphus.

Denis the Carthusian wrote a treatise, *De modo agendi processiones*, at the request of an alderman, who asked him how one might remedy the dissoluteness and debauchery to which the annual procession, in which a greatly venerated relic was borne, gave rise. "How are we to put a stop to this?" asks the alderman. "You may be sure that the town council will not easily be persuaded to abolish it, for the procession brings large profits to the town, because of all the people who have to be fed and lodged. Besides, custom will have it so." "Alas, yes," sighs Denis; "he knows too well how processions were disgraced by ribaldry, mockery and drinking." A most vivid picture of this evil is found in Chastellain's description of the degradation into which the procession of the citizens of Ghent, with the shrine of Saint Liévin, to Houthem, had fallen. Formerly, he says, the notabilities were in the habit of carrying the holy body "with great and deep solemnity and reverence"; at present there is only "a mob of roughs, and boys of bad character"; they carry it singing and yelling, "with a hundred thousand gibes, and all are drunk." They are armed, "and commit many offences where they pass, as if they were let loose and unchained; that day everything appears to be given up to them under the pretext of the body they carry."

We have already mentioned how much disturbance was caused during church services by people vying with each other in politeness. The usage of making a trysting-place of the church by young men and young women was so universal that only moralists were scandalized by it. The virtuous Christine de Pisan makes a lover say in all simplicity:

If I often go to church, It is all for seeing the fair one Fresh as a new-blown rose.

The Church suffered more serious profanation than the little love services of a young man who offered his fair one the "pax," or knelt by her side. According to the preacher Menot, prostitutes had the effrontery to come there in search of customers. Gerson tells that even in the churches and on festival days obscene pictures were sold *tanquam idola Belphegor,* which corrupted the young, while sermons were ineffective to remedy this evil.

As to pilgrimages, moralists and satirists are of one mind; people often go "pour folle plaisance." The Chevalier de la Tour Landry naïvely classes them with profane pleasures, and he entitles one of his chapters, "Of those who are fond of going to jousts and on pilgrimages."

On festal days, exclaims Nicolas de Clemanges, people go to visit distant churches, not so much to redeem a pledge of pilgrimage as to give themselves up to pleasure. Pilgrimages are the occasions of all kinds of debauchery; procurresses are always found there, people come for amorous purposes. It is a common incident in the *Quinze Joyes de Mariage;* the young wife, who wants a change, makes her husband believe that the baby is ill, because she has not yet accomplished her vow of pilgrimage, made during her confinement. The marriage of Charles VI with Isabella of Bavaria was preceded by a pilgrimage. It is far from surprising that the serious followers of the *devotio moderna* called the utility of pilgrimages in question. Those who often go on pilgrimages, says Thomas à Kempis, rarely become saints. One of his friends, Frederick of Heilo, wrote a special treatise, *Contra peregrinantes.*

The excesses and abuses resulting from an extreme familiarity with things holy, as well as the insolent mingling of pleasure with religion, are generally characteristic of periods of unshaken faith and of a deeply religious culture. The same people who in their daily life mechanically follow the routine of a rather degraded sort of worship will be capable of rising suddenly, at the ardent word of a preaching monk, to unparalleled heights of religious emotion. Even the stupid sin of blasphemy has its roots in a profound faith. It is a sort of perverted act of faith, affirming the omnipresence of God and His intervention in the minutest concerns. Only the idea of really daring Heaven gives blasphemy its sinful charm. As soon as an oath loses its character of an invocation of God, the habit of swearing changes its nature and becomes mere coarseness. At the end of the Middle Ages blasphemy is still a sort of daring diversion which belongs to the nobility. "What!" says the nobleman to the peasant in a treatise by Gerson, "you give your soul to the devil, you deny God without being noble?" Deschamps, on his part, notices that the habit of swearing tends to descend to people of low estate.

There is none so mean but says, I deny God and His mother.

People make a pastime of coining new and ingenious oaths, says Gerson: he who excels in this impious art is honoured as a master. Deschamps tells us that all France swore first after the Gascon and the English fashion, next after the Breton, and finally after the Burgundian. He composed two ballads in succession made up of all the oaths then in vogue strung together, and ended with a pious phrase. The Burgundian oath was the worst of all. It was, *Je renie Dieu* (I deny God), which was softened down to *Je renie de bottes* (boots). The Burgundians had the reputation of being abominable swearers; for the rest, says Gerson, the whole of France, for all her Christianity, suffers more than any other country from the effects of this horrible sin, which causes pestilence, war and famine. Even monks were guilty of mild swearing. Gerson and d'Ailly expressly call upon the authorities to combat the evil by renewing the strict regulations everywhere, but imposing light penalties which may be really exacted. And a royal decree of 1397, in fact, re-established the old ones of 1269 and 1347, but unfortunately also renewed the old penalties of lip-slitting and cutting out of tongues, which bore witness, it is true, to a holy horror of blasphemy, but which it was not possible to enforce. In the margin of the register containing the ordinance, someone has noted: "At present, 1411, all these oaths are in general use throughout the kingdom without being punished."

Gerson, with his long experience as a confessor, knew the psychological nature of the sin of blasphemy very well. On the one hand, he says, there are the habitual swearers, who, though culpable, are not perjurers, as it is not their intention to take an oath. On the other, we find young men of a pure and simple nature who are irresistibly tempted to blaspheme and to deny God. Their case reminds us of John Bunyan's, whose disease took the form of "a propensity to utter blasphemy, and especially to renounce his share in the benefits of the redemption." Gerson counsels these young men to give themselves up less to the contemplation of God and the saints, as they lack the mental strength required.

It is impossible to draw the line of demarcation between an ingenuous familiarity and conscious infidelity. As early as the fifteenth century people liked to show themselves *esprits forts* and to deride piety in others. The word "papelard," meaning a hypocrite, was in frequent use with lay writers of the time. "De jeune angelot vieux diable" (a young saint makes an old devil), said the proverb, or, in solemn Latin metre, *Angelicus juvenis senibus sathanizat in annis.* "It is by such sayings," Gerson exclaims, "that youth is perverted. A brazen face, scurrilous language and curses, immodest looks and gestures, are praised in children. Well, what is to be expected in old age of a *sathanizing* youth?"

The people, he says, do not know how to steer a middle course between overt unbelief and the foolish credulity, of which the clergy themselves set the example. They give credence to all revelations and prophecies, which are often but fancies of diseased people or lunatics, and yet when a serious divine, who has been honoured by genuine revelations, is occasionally mistaken, he is called impostor and "papelard," and the people henceforth refuse to listen to any divine because all are considered hypocrites.

We not unfrequently find individual expressions of avowed unbelief. "Beaux seigneurs," says Captain Bétisac to his comrades when about to die, "I have attended to my spiritual concerns and, in my conscience, I believe I have greatly angered God, having for a long time already erred against the faith, and I cannot believe a word about the Trinity, nor that the Son of God has humbled Himself to such an extent as to come down from Heaven into the carnal body of a woman; and I believe and say that when we die there is no such thing as a soul. . . . I have held this opinion ever since I became self-conscious, and I shall hold it till the end." The provost of Paris, Hugues Aubriot, is a violent hater of the clergy; he does not believe in the sacrament of the altar, he makes a mock of it; he does not keep Easter, he does not go to confession. Jacques du Clercq relates that several noblemen, in full possession of their faculties, refused extreme unction. Perhaps we should regard these isolated cases of unbelief less as wilful heresy than as a spontaneous reaction against the incessant and pressing call of the faith, arising from a culture overcharged with religious images and concepts. In any case, they should not be confounded either with the literary and superficial paganism of the Renaissance, nor with the prudent epicureanism of some aristocratic circles from the thirteenth century downward, nor, above all, with the passionate negation of ignorant heretics who had passed the boundary-line between mysticism and pantheism.

The naïve religious conscience of the multitude had no need of intellectual proofs in matters of faith. The mere presence of a visible image of things holy sufficed to establish their truth. No doubts intervened between the sight of all those pictures and statues—the persons of the Trinity, the flames of hell, the innumerable saints—and belief in their reality. All these conceptions became matters of faith in the most direct manner; they passed straight from the state of images to that of convictions, taking root in the mind as pictures clearly outlined and vividly coloured, possessing all the reality claimed for them by the Church, and even a little more.

Now, when faith is too directly connected with a pictured representation of doctrine, it runs the risk of no longer making qualitative distinctions between the nature and the degree of sanctity of the different elements of religion. The image by itself does not teach the faithful that one should adore God and only venerate the saints. Its psychological function is limited to creating a deep conviction of reality and a lively feeling of respect. It therefore became the task of the Church to warn incessantly against want of discrimination in this respect, and to preserve the purity of doctrine by explaining precisely what the image stood for. In no other sphere was the danger of luxuriance of religious thought caused by a vivid imagination more obvious.

Now, the Church did not fail to teach that all honours rendered to the saints, to relics, to holy places, should have God for their object. Although the prohibition of images in the second commandment of the Decalogue was abrogated by the new law, or limited to God the Father alone, the Church purposed, nevertheless, to maintain intact the principle of *non adorabis ea neque coles:* Images were only meant to show simple-minded people what to believe. They are the books of the illiterate, says Clemanges; a thought which Villon has expressed in the touching lines which he puts into his mother's mouth:

I am a poor old woman who knows nothing; I never could read. In my parish church I see Paradise painted, where are harps and lutes, And a hell, where the damned are boiled. The one frightens me, the other brings joy and mirth.

The medieval Church was, however, rather heedless of the danger of a deterioration of the faith caused by the popular imagination roaming unchecked in the sphere of hagiology. An abundance of pictorial fancy, after all, furnished to the simple mind quite as much matter for deviating from pure doctrine as any personal interpretation of Holy Scripture. It is remarkable that the Church, so scrupulous in dogmatic matters, should have been so confiding and indulgent towards those who, sinning out of ignorance, rendered more homage to images than was lawful. It suffices, says Gerson, that they meant to do as the Church requires.

Thus towards the end of the Middle Ages an ultra-realistic conception of all that related to the saints may be noticed in the popular faith. The saints had become so real and such familiar characters of current religion that they became bound up with all the more superficial religious impulses. While profound devotion still centred on Christ and His mother, quite a host of artless beliefs and fancies clustered about the saints. Everything contributed to make them familiar and life-like. They were dressed like the people themselves. Every day one met "Messires" Saint Roch and Saint James in the persons of living plague patients and pilgrims. Down to the Renaissance

the costume of the saints always followed the fashion of the times. Only then did Sacred Art, by arraying the saints in classical draperies, withdraw them from the popular imagination and place them in a sphere where the fancy of the multitude could no longer contaminate the doctrine in its purity.

The distinctly corporeal conception of the saints was accentuated by the veneration of their relics, not only permitted by the Church but forming an integral part of religion. It was inevitable that this pious attachment to material things should draw all hagiolatry into a sphere of crude and primitive ideas, and lead to surprising extremes. In the matter of relics the deep and straightforward faith of the Middle Ages was never afraid of disillusionment or profanation through handling holy things coarsely. The spirit of the fifteenth century did not differ much from that of the Umbrian peasants, who, about the year 1000, wished to kill Saint Romuald, the hermit, in order to make sure of his precious bones; or of the monks of Fossanuova, who, after Saint Thomas Aquinas had died in their monastery, in their fear of losing the relic, did not shrink from decapitating, boiling and preserving the body. During the lying in state of Saint Elizabeth of Hungary, in 1231, a crowd of worshippers came and cut or tore strips of the linen enveloping her face; they cut off the hair, the nails, even the nipples. In 1392, King Charles VI of France, on the occasion of a solemn feast, was seen to distribute ribs of his ancestor, Saint Louis; to Pierre d'Ailly and to his uncles Berry and Burgundy he gave entire ribs; to the prelates one bone to divide between them, which they proceeded to do after the meal.

It may well be that this too corporeal

and familiar aspect, this too clearly out-lined shape, of the saints has been the very reason why they occupy so little space in the sphere of visions and super-natural experience. The whole domain of ghost-seeing, signs, spectres and apparitions, so crowded in the Middle Ages, lies mainly apart from the vener-ation of the saints. Of course, there are exceptions, such as Saint Michael, Saint Katherine and Saint Margaret appearing to Joan of Arc, and other instances might be added. But, generally speak-ing, popular phantasmagoria is full of angels, devils, shades of the dead, white women, but not of saints. Stories of ap-paritions of particular saints are, as a rule, suspect of having already under-gone some ecclesiastical or literary interpretation. To the agitated beholder a phantom has no name and hardly a shape. In the famous vision of Franken-thal, in 1446, the young shepherd *sees* fourteen cherubim, all alike, who *tell* him they are the fourteen "Holy Mar-tyrs," to whom Christian iconography attributed such distinct and marked appearances. Where a primitive super-stition does attach to the veneration of some saint, it retains something of the vague and formless character that is essential to superstition, as in the case of Saint Bertulph at Ghent, who can be heard rapping the sides of his coffin in St. Peter's abbey "moult dru et moult fort" (very frequently and very loudly) as a warning of impending calamity.

The saint, with his clearly outlined figure, his well-known attributes and features as they were painted or carved in the churches, was wholly lacking in mystery. He did not inspire terror as do vague phantoms and the haunting unknown. The dread of the supernatural is due to the undefined character of its phenomena. As soon as they assume a clear-cut shape they are no longer hor-rible. The familiar figures of the saints produced the same sort of reassuring effect as the sight of a policeman in a foreign city. The complex of ideas con-nected with the saints constituted, so to say, a neutral zone of calm and domes-tic piety, between the ecstasy of contem-plation and of the love of Christ on the one hand, and the horrors of demon-omania on the other. It is perhaps not too bold to assert that the veneration of the saints, by draining off an overflow of religious effusion and of holy fear, acted on the exuberant piety of the Middle Ages as a salutary sedative.

The veneration of the saints has its place among the more outward mani-festations of faith. It is subject to the influences of popular fancy rather than of theology, and they sometimes deprive it of its dignity. The special cult of Saint Joseph towards the end of the Middle Ages is characteristic in this respect. It may be looked upon as the counterpart of the passionate adoration of the Virgin. The curiosity with which Joseph was regarded is a sort of reaction from the fervent cult of Mary. The figure of the Virgin is exalted more and more and that of Joseph becomes more and more of a caricature. Art portrays him as a clown dressed in rags; as such he appears in the diptych by Melchior Broederlam at Dijon. Literature, which is always more explicit than the graphic arts, achieves the feat of making him altogether ridiculous. Instead of admir-ing Joseph as the man most highly fav-oured of all, Deschamps represents him as the type of the drudging husband.

You who serve a wife and children Always bear Joseph in mind; He served his wife,

gloomily and mournfully, And he guarded
Jesus Christ in his infancy; He went on foot
with his bundle slung on his staff; In several
places he is pictured thus, Beside a mule to
give them pleasure, And so he had never any
amusement in this world.

And again, still more grossly:

What poverty Joseph suffered What hard-
ships What misery When God was born! Many
a time he has carried him, And placed him
In his goodness With his mother, too, On
his mule, and took them with him: I saw him
Painted thus; He went into Egypt.
The good man is painted Quite exhausted,
And dressed in A frock and a striped garment,
A stick across his shoulder, Old, spent And
broken. For him there was no amusement in
this world, But of him People say—That is
Joseph, the fool.

This shows how familiarity led to
irreverence of thought. Saint Joseph
remained a comic type, in spite of the
very special reverence paid to him.
Doctor Eck, Luther's adversary, had to
insist that he should not be brought on
the stage, or at least that he should not
be made to cook the porridge, *"ne ecclesia
Dei irrideatur."* The union of Joseph and
Mary always remained the object of a
deplorable curiosity, in which profane
speculation mingled with sincere piety.
The Chevalier de la Tour Landry, a man
of prosaic mind, explains it to himself
in the following manner: "God wished
that she should marry that saintly man
Joseph, who was old and upright, for
God wished to be born in wedlock, to
comply with the current legal requirements, to avoid gossip."
An unpublished work of the fifteenth
century represents the mystic marriage
of the soul with the celestial spouse as
if it were a middle-class wedding. "If
it pleases you," says Jesus to the Father,

"I shall marry and shall have a large
bevy of children and relations." The
Father fears a misalliance, but the Angel
succeeds in persuading him that the
betrothed-elect is worthy of the Son; on
which the Father gives his consent in
these terms:

Take her, for she is pleasing and fit To love
her sweet bridegroom; Now take plenty of
our possessions, And give them to her in
abundance.

There is no doubt of the seriously devout
intention of this treatise. It is only an
instance of the degree of triviality entailed by unbridled exuberance of fancy.
Every saint, by the possession of a
distinct and vivid outward shape, had
his own marked individuality, quite contrary to the angels, who, with the exception of the three famous archangels,
acquired no definite appearance. This
individual character of each saint was
still more strongly accentuated by the
special functions attributed to many of
them. Now this specialization of the
kind of aid given by the various saints
was apt to introduce a mechanical element into the veneration paid to them.
If, for instance, Saint Roch is specially
invoked against the plague, almost inevi-
tably too much stress came to be laid
on his part in the healing, and the idea
required by sound doctrine, that the saint
wrought the cure only be means of his
intercession with God, came in danger
of being lost sight of. This was especially
so in the case of the "Holy Martyrs"
(les saints auxiliaires), whose number is
usually given as fourteen, and sometimes
as five, eight, ten, fifteen. Their veneration arose and spread towards the end
of the Middle Ages.

There are five saints in the genealogy,
And five female saints to whom God granted

Benignantly at the end of their lives, That whosoever shall invoke their help with all his heart In all dangers, that He will hear their prayers, In all disorders whatsoever. He therefore is wise who serves these five, George, Denis, Christopher, Giles and Blaise.

The Church had sanctioned the popular belief expressed by Deschamps in these verses by instituting an office of the Fourteen Auxiliary Saints. The binding character of their intercession is clearly there expressed: "O God, who hast distinguished Thy chosen saints, George, etc., etc., with special privileges before all others, that all those who in their need invoke their help, shall obtain the salutary fulfilment of their prayer, according to the promise of Thy grace." So there had been a formal delegation of divine omnipotence. The people could, therefore not be blamed if, with regard to these privileged saints it forgot the pure doctrine a little. The instantaneous effect of prayer addressed to them contributed still more to obscure their part as intercessors; they seemed to be exercising divine power by virtue of a power of attorney. Hence it is very natural that the Church abolished this special office of the Fourteen Auxiliary Saints after the Council of Trent. The extraordinary function attributed to them had given rise to the grossest superstition, such as the belief that it sufficed to have looked at a Saint Christopher, painted or carved, to be protected for the rest of the day from a fatal end. This explains the countless number of the saints' images at the entrances of churches.

As for the reason why this group was singled out among all the saints, it should be noticed that the greater number of them appear in art with some very striking attribute. Saint Achatius wore a crown of thorns; Saint Giles was accompanied by a hind, Saint George by a dragon; Saint Christopher was of gigantic stature; Saint Blaise was represented in a den of wild beasts; Saint Cyriac with a chained devil; Saint Denis carrying his head under his arm; Saint Erasmus being disembowelled by means of a windlass; Saint Eustace with a stag carrying a cross between its antlers; Saint Pantaleon with a lion; Saint Vitus in a cauldron; Saint Barbara with her tower; Saint Katherine with her wheel and sword; Saint Margaret with a dragon. It may well be that the special favour with which the Fourteen Auxiliary Saints were regarded was due, at least partially, to the very impressive character of their images.

The names of several saints were inseparably bound up with divers disorders, and even served to designate them. Thus various cutaneous diseases were called Saint Anthony's evil. Gout went by the name of Saint Maur's evil. The terrors of the plague called for more than one saintly protector; Saint Sebastian, Saint Roch, Saint Giles, Saint Christopher, Saint Valentine, Saint Adrian, were all honoured in this capacity by offices, processions and fraternities. Now here lurked another menace to the purity of the faith. As soon as the thought of the disease, charged with feelings of horror and fear, presented itself to the mind, the thought of the saint sprang up at the same instant. How easily, then, did the saint himself become the object of this fear, so that to him was ascribed the heavenly wrath that unchained the scourge. Instead of unfathomable divine justice, it was the anger of the saint which seemed the cause of the evil and required to be appeased. Since he healed the evil, why should he not be its author? On these lines the transition from Christian ethic to heathen magic was only too easy. The Church could not be held responsible, unless we are to blame her carelessness regarding the adulteration of the pure doctrine in the minds of the ignorant.

There are numerous testimonies to show that the people sometimes really regarded certain saints as the authors of disorders, though it would be hardly fair to consider as such those oaths which almost attributed to Saint Anthony the part of an evil fire-demon. "Que Saint Antoine me arde" (May Saint Anthony burn me!), "Saint Antoine arde le tripot," "Saint Antoine arde la monture" (Saint Anthony burn the brothel! Saint Anthony burn the beast!)—these are lines by Coquillart. So also Deschamps makes some poor fellow say:

"Saint Anthony sells me his evil all too dear, He stokes the fire in my body."

and thus apostrophizes a gouty beggar: "You cannot walk? All the better, you save the toll: Saint Mor ne te fera fremir" (Saint Maur will not make you tremble).

Robert Gaguin, who was not at all hostile to the veneration of the saints, in his *De validorum per Franciam mendicantium varia astucia,* describes beggars in these terms: "One falls on the ground expectorating malodorous spittle and attributes his condition to Saint John. Others are covered with ulcers through the fault of Saint Fiacrius, the hermit. You, O Damian, prevent them from making water, Saint Anthony burns their joints, Saint Pius makes them lame and paralysed."

In one of his Colloquies Erasmus makes fun of this belief. One of the interlocutors asks whether in Heaven the saints are more malevolent than they were on earth. "Yes," answers the other, "in the glory of Paradise the saints do not choose to be insulted. Who was sweeter than

Saint Corneille, more compassionate than Saint Anthony, more patient than Saint John the Baptist, during their lives? And now what horrible maladies they send if they are not properly honoured!" Rabelais states that the lower class of preachers themselves represented Saint Sebastian to their congregation as the author of the plague and Saint Eutropius of dropsy. Henri Estienne has written of the same superstitions in the like manner. That they existed is thus clearly established.

The emotional constituents of the veneration of the saints had fastened so firmly on the forms and colours of their images that mere aesthetic perception was constantly threatening to obliterate the religious element. The vivid impression presented by the aspect of the images with their pious or ecstatic looks, rich gilding, and sumptuous apparel, all admirably reproduced by a very realistic art, left hardly any room for doctrinal reflection. Effusions of piety went out ardently towards those glorious beings, without a thought being given to the limits fixed by the Church. In the popular imagination the saints were living and were as gods. There is nothing surprising, therefore, in the fact that strict pietists like the Brethren of the Common Life and the Windesheim canons saw a certain danger to popular piety in the development of the veneration of the saints. It is very remarkable, however, that the same idea occurs to a man like Eustache Deschamps, a superficial poet and a commonplace mind, and for that very reason so faithful a mirror of the general aspirations of his time.

Do not make gods of silver, Of gold, of wood, of stone or of bronze, That lead people to idolatry. . . . Because the work has a pleasant shape; Their colouring of which I complain, The beauty of shining gold, Make many ignorant people believe That these are God for certain, And they serve by foolish thoughts Such images as stand about In churches where they place too many of them That is very ill done; in short Let us not adore such counterfeits. . . .

Prince, let us only believe in one God And let us adore him to perfection In the fields, everywhere, for this is right, No false gods, of iron or of stone, Stones which have no understanding: Let us not adore such counterfeits.

Perhaps we may consider the diligent propagation of the cult of guardian angels towards the end of the Middle Ages as a sort of unconscious reaction against the motley crowd of popular hagiology. Too large a part of the living faith had crystallized in the veneration of the saints, and thus there arose a craving for something more spiritual as an object of reverence and a source of protection. In addressing itself to the angel, vaguely conceived and almost formless, piety restored contact with the supernatural and with mystery. Once more it is Jean Gerson, the indefatigable worker for the purity of faith, whom we find perpetually recommending the cult of the guardian angel. But here also he had to combat unbridled curiosity, which threatened to submerge piety under a mass of commonplace details. And it was just in connection with this subject of angels, which was more or less unbroken ground, that numbers of delicate ques-

tions obtruded themselves. Do they never leave us? Do they know beforehand whether we shall be saved or lost? Had Christ a guardian angel? Will the Antichrist have one? Can the angel speak to our soul without visions? Do the angels lead us to good as devils lead us to evil?— Leave these subtle speculations to divines, concludes Gerson; let the faithful keep to simple and wholesome worship.

A hundred years after Gerson wrote, the Reformation attacked the cult of the saints, and nowhere in the whole contested area did it meet with less resistance. In strong contrast with the belief in witchcraft and demonology, which fully maintained their ground in Protestant countries, both among the clergy and the laity, the saints fell without a blow being struck in their defence. This was possibly due to the fact that nearly everything connected with the saints had become *caput mortuum*. Piety had depleted itself in the image, the legend, the office. All its contents had been so completely expressed that mystic awe had evaporated. The cult of the saints was no longer rooted in the domain of the unimaginable. In the case of demonology, these roots remained as terribly strong as ever.

When, therefore, Catholic Reform had to re-establish the cult of the saints, its first task was to prune it; to cut down the whole luxuriant growth of medieval imagination and establish severer discipline, so as to prevent a reflorescence.

Suggested Additional Readings

This list includes mainly works that are available in English, and it is limited largely to the topics treated in the book. I have made no attempt to make the list exhaustive even according to the above criteria, and some instructors will probably find that their favorite study has been omitted.

Owen Chadwick, *The History of the Church: A Select Bibliography*, 2nd ed. (London, 1966) is an easily available work which will be useful to students who want to pursue studies in various aspects of Church history on their own. There are many surveys of early Church history. L. Duchesne, *Early History of the Christian Church*, 3 vols. (London, 1909–1924) is one of the most comprehensive, and *Henry Chadwick, *The Early Church* (Baltimore, 1967) is one of the most recent. When it is finally completed, the best general history is likely to be J. Danielou and H. Marrou, eds., *Christian Centuries* (London, 1964–   ). At present the best general treatment of the medieval Church is A. Fliche and E. Martin, eds., *Histoire de l 'Eglise*, (Paris, 1935–   ).

On the success and organization of the early Church, see K. S. Latourette, *A History of the Expansion of Christianity*, 7 vols. (New York, 1937–1945); *H. O. Taylor, *The Emergence of Christian Culture in the West* (New York, 1961); *H. Lietzmann, *A History of the Early Church*, 4 vols. (London, 1949–1951); and *F. Van der Meer, *Augustine the Bishop* (New York, 1961). For those who would pursue the subject in German, E. Caspar, *Geschichte des Papsttums*, 2 vols. (Tübingen, 1930–1933) and H. von Schubert, *Geschichte der christlichen Kirche im Frümittelalter* (Tübingen, 1921) are fundamental works.

For the role played by the Church among the barbarians, see *J. M. Wallace-Hadrill, *The Barbarian West* (New York, 1962); A. K. Ziegler, *Church and State in Visigothic Spain* (Washington, 1930); W. Levison, *England and the Continent in the Eighth Century* (London, 1946); T. Schieffer, *Winfrid-Bonifatius und die christliche Grundlegung Europas* (Freiburg im Breisgau, 1954); E. Caspar, *Das Papsttum unter fränkischer Herrschaft* (Darmstadt, 1956); and L. Halphen, *Charlemagne et l'empire carolingien* (Paris, 1947). The most comprehensive survey of Church thinkers in this period is *M. L. W. Laistner, *Thought and Letters in Western Europe 500–900* (Ithaca, N.Y., 1957). Of general value is *E. K. Rand, *The Founders of the Middle Ages* (Cambridge, Mass., 1928). For detailed study of specific aspects of Church thought, see two books by K. F. Morrison, *The Two Kingdoms* (Princeton, N.J., 1964) and *Tradition and Authority in the Western Church, 300–1140* (Princeton, N.J., 1969).

The development of the Papacy and the reform of the Church are treated by A. Fliche, *La réforme grégorienne*, 3 vols. (Louvain, 1924–1937); J. G. Jalland, *The Church and the Papacy* (London, 1944); W. T. Ullmann, *The Growth of Papal Government in the Middle Ages* (London, 1968); Z. N. Brooke, *The English Church and the Papacy*, 2nd ed. (London, 1952); J. B. Russell, *Dissent and Reform in the Early Middle Ages* (Los Angeles, 1965); and *G. Barraclough, *The Medieval Papacy* (New York, 1968). See also *R. W. Southern, *The Making of the Middle Ages* (New Haven, Conn., 1967).

On the investiture struggle and its aftermath, see J. P. Whitney, *Hildebrandline Essays* (London, 1932); M. Pacaut, *Alexandre*

---

*Astericks indicate works available in paperback.

III. *Étude sur la conception du pouvoir pontifical dans sa pensée et dans son oeuvre* (Paris, 1956). E. N. Johnson, *Secular Activities of the German Episcopate: 919–1024* (Lincoln, Nebr., 1930–1931) provides good background material on Germany, and N. Cantor, *Church, Kingship, and Lay Investiture in England 1089–1135* (Princeton, N.J., 1958) treats the conflict itself in England. See also W. T. Ullmann, *Medieval Papalism* (London, 1949); K. Wenck, "Die römischen Päpste zwischen Alexander III. und Innocenz III.," in A. Brackmann, ed. *Papsttum und Kaisertum* (Munich, 1926); L. E. Binns, *Innocent III* (London, 1931); and A. Luchaire, *Innocent III,* 6 vols. (Paris, 1905–1908).

On the Crusades (aside from Runciman's work which is quoted in the text), see K. M. Setton, ed., *A History of the Crusades,* 5 vols. projected, which is likely to become the most important work in English; available now are: vol. 1, *The First Hundred Years* (Philadelphia, 1955) and vol. 2, *The Later Crusades* (Philadelphia, 1962). In French, see R. Grousset, *Histoire des croisades et du royaume franc de Jérusalem,* 3 vols. (Paris, 1934–1936). A brief but useful survey is *R. A. Newhall, *The Crusades,* rev. ed. (New York, 1963). Other works to consult are: A. S. Atiya, *The Crusade in the Later Middle Ages* (London, 1938) and *Crusade, Commerce, and Culture* (Bloomington, Ind., 1962); also D. C. Munro, *Kingdom of the Crusaders* (New York, 1936) and E. Barker, *The Crusades* (London, 1923), a brief survey. On special aspects, see C. Erdmann, *Die Entstehung der Kreuzzugsgedanken* (Stuttgart, 1935); M. Melville, *La vie des Templiers* (Paris, 1951); and E. J. King, *The Knights Hospitallers in the Holy Land* (London, 1931). The student who would pursue more detailed interests in the Crusades should consult A. S. Atiya, *The Crusade: Historiography and Bibliography* (Bloomington, Ind., 1962).

On the Church and medieval culture, see *C. H. Haskins, *The Renaissance of the 12th Century* (Cambridge, Mass., 1927): H. O. Taylor, *The Mediaeval Mind,* 2 vols. (Cambridge, Mass., 1926); F. B. Artz, *The Mind of the Middle Ages,* 3rd ed. (New York, 1962); E. Gilson, *Héloïse and Abelard* (Chicago,

1951); D. Knowles, *The Evolution of Medieval Thought* (New York, 1962); *A. O. Lovejoy, *The Great Chain of Being* (Cambridge, Mass., 1936); and L. Thorndike, *A History of Magic and Experimental Science,* 6 vols. (New York, 1958). On the universities, see H. Rashdall, *The Universities of Europe in the Middle Ages,* 3 vols., rev. ed. (London, 1936) and R. S. Rait, *Life in the Medieval University* (London, 1912). Of great general value is R. L. Poole, *Illustrations of the History of Medieval Thought and Learning,* 2nd ed. (London, 1920).

Some useful essays on the Church and economics in the Middle Ages are to be found in J. H. Clapham et al., eds. *The Cambridge Economic History* (London, 1941–1961), vols. 1–3. An old but important work is W. Endemann, *Studien in der romanischkanonistische Wirtschafts- und Rechtslehre,* 2 vols. (Berlin, 1874–1883). On Church economy, see W. E. Lunt, *Papal Revenues in the Middle Ages,* 2 vols. (New York, 1934) and *Financial Relations of the Papacy with England to 1327* (Cambridge, Mass., 1939); Y. Renouard, *Les relations des papes d'Avignon et des compagnies commerciales et bancaires de 1316 à 1378* (Paris, 1941); and Ch. Samaran and G. Mollat, *La fiscalité pontificale en France au XIVe siècle* (Paris, 1905). On the important topic of usury, see B. N. Nelson, *The Idea of Usury* (Princeton, N.J., 1949); T. MacLaughlin, "The Teaching of the Canonists on Usury," *Medieval Studies,* I (1939) and IV (1944); and J. T. Noonan, *The Scholastic Analysis of Usury* (Cambridge, Mass., 1957). On banking, see R. De Roover, *The Rise and Decline of the Medici Bank, 1397-1494* (Cambridge, Mass., 1963) and *Money, Banking and Credit in Mediaeval Bruges* (Cambridge, Mass., 1948); and A. B. Kerr, *Jacques Couer* (New York, 1928). On Church property, see J. A. Raftis, *The Estates of Ramsey Abbey* (Toronto, 1957); W. H. Doheny, *Church Property: Modes of Acquisition* (Washington, 1927); and E. Lesne, *Histoire de la propriété ecclésiastique en France,* 6 vols. (Lille, 1910–1943).

The decline of the Church and the disintegration of medieval society are discussed in L. E. Binns, *The Decline and Fall of the*

Medieval Papacy (London, 1934) and A. C. Flick, *The Decline of the Medieval Church* (New York, 1930). See also G. Mollat, *The Popes at Avignon* (New York, 1965); *H.·B. Workman, *John Wyclif: a Study of the English Medieval Church* (Hamden, Conn., 1966); H. Kaminsky, *A History of the Hussite Revolution* (Los Angeles, 1967); and *N. Cohn, *The Pursuit of the Millennium* 2nd ed. (New York, 1970). See also J. Rivière, *Le problème de l'église et de l'état au temps de Philippe le Bel* (Louvain, 1926); E. Kraack, *Rom oder Avignon* (Marburg, 1929); W. T. Ullmann, *The Origins of the Great Schism* (London, 1948); B. Tierney, *Foundations of the Conciliar Theory* (London, 1955); and J. Guiraud, *L'église romaine et les origines de la renaissance,* 5th ed. (Paris, 1921).